D0100005

LISTEN

LISTEN

Finding God in the Story of Your Life

KERI WYATT KENT

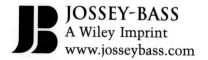

JOSSEY-BASS
A Wiley Imprint
www.josseybass.com

Published by Jossey-Bass

A Wiley Imprint

989 Market Street, San Francisco, CA 94103-1741   www.josseybass.com

Jossey-Bass books and products are available through most bookstores. To contact Jossey-Bass directly, call our Customer Care Department within the U.S. at 800-956-7739, outside the U.S. at 317-572-3986, or fax 317-572-4002.

Jossey-Bass also publishes its books in a variety of electronic formats. Some content that appears in print may not be available in electronic books.

Library of Congress Cataloging-in-Publication Data

Kent, Keri Wyatt

Listen: finding God in the story of your life / Keri Wyatt Kent.

p. cm.

Includes bibliographical references.

ISBN-10: 0-7879-8233-4 (alk. paper)

ISBN-13: 978-0-7879-8233-1 (alk. paper)

1. Spiritual biography. 2. Listening—Religious aspects. I. Title.

BL624.K465 2005

248.4—dc22   2005033964

Printed in the United States of America

FIRST EDITION

HB Printing 10 9 8 7 6 5 4 3 2 1

Contents

∽ v ∾

Acknowledgments

I could not have written about listening if I had not experienced for myself the ministry of listening. Many friends have offered me this kindness. I am especially grateful for the deep listening offered me in spiritual friendship with Sibyl Towner, Ruth Barton, Jim and Debbie Pio, Lynn Siewert, and Deb Poling. In different voices, in different seasons, I have heard God through each of you.

Thank you to my family—Scot, Melanie, and Aaron—for giving me time and space to write and for challenging me to stop writing often enough to live out what I'm writing about.

Thanks to agents Chip MacGregor and Beth Jusino for encouraging me and guiding the process from start to finish.

Thanks also to Bob Gordon, who not only edited but helped me find the direction the book needed to go.

Also, thank you to Ken Gire, who gave me a word of encouragement at just the right time.

LISTEN

Introduction

Paying Attention

There is ecstasy in paying attention.
—ANNE LAMOTT[1]

I t was Veterans Day, raw and windy. I hurried into the grocery store to get a few things. A man a few years older than I sat outside, collecting coins in exchange for shiny little paper poppies. I don't remember how—perhaps he held a hand-lettered cardboard sign, or maybe I just read his age and his hardened face—but I knew that he had served in Vietnam.

I fished in my purse for a dollar. He sat in his second-hand lawn chair and silently held up a plastic box so I could slide the money through the slot in the top, then handed me the tiny red paper-and-wire flower. The wind made my eyes tear, and I hurried into the store.

As I power-walked the aisles and tossed cereal, fish sticks, and pasta into my cart, I thought about the veteran outside. What had his life been before that long-ago war? What had he done with his life in the years since? What had it been like to come back to a country divided by protests over the war in which he'd lost his buddies? Had he been confronted or criticized for what he'd done? Did he have memories of "flower children" holding peace signs while yelling at him? There was a certain irony to his handing out flowers.

I averted my gaze as I walked out of the store. I'm not sure why. I loaded the groceries into the back of the van and then sat in the driver's seat. Go back, something told me. Say something. Acknowledge him.

Since I've been trying to listen to God, and to my life, I thought there must be something God wanted me to learn, some holy moment I would experience if I obeyed that little voice in my head.

I drove my minivan up to the pick-up lane and put it in park. I sat there for a minute, then got out, leaving it idling. I went up to the grizzled man. "Sir?" He looked up. "Thank you," I told him. "Really. Thanks for what you've done."

I don't know what I expected. A gush of emotion? A smile? I got neither. "Yeah," he said softly, but his face was still as hard, as guarded. "Okay." He might as well have added "whatever" and rolled his eyes.

I felt suddenly awkward, stupid. What was I thinking? Was it God who told me to say something or was it just a stupid idea that popped into my head? If it was God, why wasn't I getting some kind of affirmation? Then again, what exactly was I looking for?

"Good-bye," I said. He only nodded, looking away.

I got back in the van and drove away. I wish I could tell you that I later received some deep revelation as a result of listening to that leading and acting on it. I didn't. It was just a time where I practiced paying attention and practiced obeying. I don't know the result. But that's not something I need to know. It may be that the only result was that a tired old vet thought I was goofy, or worse, that I had no stinking idea what he had been through. That doesn't matter. What I'm working on is learning how to pay attention, to listen to my life and see if God's speaking through it.

Looking back, I am beginning to see the result, not for the vet but for me. I think God wants me to know that I have no idea of the depths of other people's suffering, and I may never have any idea what my simple act of paying attention did for that man. *And I don't need to know what it did for him.* I know what it did for me.

It gave me a good practice session on giving without expecting anything in return.

Jesus said we ought to love indiscriminately. To elaborate, he added, "And if you lend to those from whom you expect repayment, what credit is that to you? Even 'sinners' lend to 'sinners,' expecting to be repaid in full" (Luke 6:34, *The Message*[2]). Whether we are giving money or a kind word, Jesus invites us to be generous and kind without any thought of payback, or even appreciation. It's part of following him.

I tell you: love your enemies. Help and give without expecting a return. Jesus continued in that passage, according to Eugene Peterson's paraphrase, by saying, "You'll never—I promise—regret it. Live out this God-created identity the way our Father lives toward us, generously and graciously, even when we're at our worst. Our Father is kind; you be kind" (Luke 6:35–36).

I claim to be a follower of Jesus. There was a time in my life when he wooed me, and I could not resist him. Since then, I've simply tried to love him, and he's done an amazing job of loving me. While my faithfulness sometimes wavered, his never did. He's *in* my life, not just a part of it, but all of it. So listening to my life, by definition, means listening to Jesus. It means paying attention to all that I feel or think or experience, because Jesus is using it to help me, as Peterson puts it, "live out this God-created identity."

What does it mean, to pay attention? The word *pay* implies a cost. And there is one. I must give up trying to hear all voices and tune in to just one. I must forsake the loud shouts of my own needs, my doubts, my fears, and move toward the one I am offering my attention to, the one I am called to listen to.

What would happen to you if you learned how to really listen—how to listen to God through your life, through other people, and through spiritual practices? And not just to gain information, because we already have plenty of information. Ask yourself: What if I could listen, not just to get good at a skill but for the purpose of transforming my life and relationships? What would happen to you as a person if you knew that you were heard, and loved, and that you had the ability to love and listen to others?

This book is about learning to really listen and becoming transformed by what we hear, all the while knowing God always hears us and completely understands the pleadings of our hearts.

So, how do we learn to listen? Before we begin, we must truly believe that God speaks. Jan Johnson writes:

> *Many people believe God no longer speaks to us today.* Some Christians insist that two-way exchanges with the Father no longer occur. They believe that anything the Bible says about listening to God or the guidance of the Holy Spirit applied only to a certain time in history.[3]

Yes, some people still believe that God does not speak to us directly. But others might go to the other extreme and think that every thought in our head is a message from God. And I'm confident that's not true, either.

It is possible to listen to God. It takes discipline, motivated by love. It takes discernment to figure out which thoughts are from God and which are just our own rationalizing or wishful thinking. But I know sometimes I go through life not really paying attention. And I'm thinking that faith, that loving God, is about really noticing what he's doing and saying. Scott Peck writes: "The principal form that the work of love takes is attention. . . . By far the most common and important way in which we can exercise our attention is by listening."[4]

The work of love requires us to pay attention. As we learn to pay attention, we will begin to live the way we were meant to live.

"People are meant to live in an ongoing conversation with God, speaking and being spoken to," writes Dallas Willard.[5] That's what you were made for: conversation with God. "Of course talking *to* God is an almost universal practice."

But, Willard continues, hearing *from* God is often a suspect practice. Maybe we think God might have once spoken to us, but we're not sure. Or we don't want to talk about it, because people won't believe us or will think we are odd, or worse. We let our "reason" decide that we can't hear from someone we can't see. We know people who say they've heard from God, and we sometimes wonder if what they say is really true, or if they are simply trying to manipulate us by citing God's authority.

I believe many of us have a one-sided relationship with God. We talk much more than we listen. Something's missing. I want to learn how to listen to God.

God is perfectly able to communicate in a million ways, but we often do not hear, or we

> *Most of us prefer listening to a pastor or speaker rather than training ourselves to sit in quiet and listen to God.*
>
> —JAN JOHNSON[6]

ignore what we hear. We start to say, "Oh, I get it," but then we doubt, or worse, we get logical and try to explain the unexplainable. "It's just the wind . . . it's just my own neuroses talking . . . it's just my imagination." As if God did not direct the wind, as if God could not redeem our neuroses or speak to us through our creative imagination.

Certainly, there are other voices in our heads besides God's, and one of the hardest things to do is to discern exactly who is talking. Figuring that out is part of what listening is all about. Thankfully, listening is both an art and a craft—both a gift to receive and a skill to hone.

Jesus often said, "He who has ears to hear, let him hear." Listening is a spiritual discipline.

How do you listen to God, to engage in the discipline of listening? I think it begins with noticing God in the story of your life—what has happened so far. Your accomplishments, your struggles, and your desires are all important elements in your story. I think God might also speak to us through other people—he can touch our hearts and shape our lives through the words of others and allow us to do that for others by what we say and how we listen to them. I'm also learning that certain practices have been helpful in enhancing and strengthening my private conversations with God. So this book is about listening to your life, listening to others, and listening through spiritual practices. These three areas are not the only ways to listen to God but are simply threads to weave into the tapestry of our life with God.

Come, let us listen to God!

 Which is easier—listening to a speaker or just sitting in quiet? Which do you prefer? How often do you sit in quiet? What feeling does the thought of doing so evoke in you? How do you feel about the idea of listening to God?

PART I

HOLY MOMENTS: LISTENING TO YOUR LIFE

Put your ear down next to your soul, and listen hard.
—ATTRIBUTED TO ANNE SEXTON[1]

The hard part about paying attention to your life is that it is filled with many voices, often with conflicting messages. The big question that needs to be asked is: What is my life saying?

"Before you tell your life what you intend to do with it, listen for what it intends to do with you," writes Parker Palmer. ". . . Vocation does not come from willfulness. It comes from listening. I must listen to my life and try to understand what it is truly about—quite apart from what I would like it to be about—or my life will never represent anything real in the world, no matter how earnest my intentions."[2]

Grand words, great idea. But you know what I'm wondering? How do you listen to your life when it feels consumed with laundry and errands and carpools? With scrubbing and wiping? With deadlines and messes and occasional arguments with the people you love? With trying to fit work and kids and even the deeper things of life into a crowded calendar? How am I supposed to listen in the midst of all that? Who cares what my life wants to do with me when I'm more worried about losing that last five pounds or getting the kids to soccer practice than I am about finding my grand purpose in the universe?

Whether or not my purpose is grand or ordinary, I'm realizing that I want to know what it is. I need to know that Someone cares and is guiding me, that my life will matter. I want to listen.

We're going to give our attention in the next three chapters to just three questions:

1. What do I love?
2. Where have I struggled?
3. What do I desire?

I believe God speaks to us about our lives through our joys, our pain, our longing, and our awareness of them will help us understand who God is and whom he has made us to be—what our life is "truly about."

CHAPTER I

What Do I Love?

Think about your life story. When did you experience joy? Galatians 5:23 says that one of the results of God's Spirit working in our life is that we will have joy. What brings you joy?

My son recently made a birthday card for a friend. "In joy your birthday," he wrote at the top, and drew a picture of a cake with candles, guarded by a Lego Bionicle warrior. He, of course, meant "enjoy," but really, he may have been on to something. If you enjoy something, you're "in joy." Right?

What puts you "in joy"? Do you ever experience joy? Did you experience it as a kid or a young person? How about lately? The things that bring you joy, that you love, will tell you about yourself, about your story. Looking at what brings you joy is a good first step toward listening to your life. By noticing what brings you joy, you get a picture of the unique way that God created you.

A lot of people I talk to seem to think that the fun stuff of life and the God stuff are in two different little compartments. This is dangerous thinking, because if that's true, why would anyone want to live a life of faith for very long? The things that bring you joy—real joy—are gifts from God. God has been involved in the story of your life from the beginning, whether you noticed or acknowledged that or not. So if you notice—Where have I felt joy? What things do I love?—you can notice God. Because those things are gifts from God; they are things to pay attention to because God speaks through them.

Listening to your life has a purpose. You listen to it so that you can take who you are and put it into what you do. Jesus said he came that our joy would be full. Knowing what you love, noticing the blessings of God—that is the beginning of listening to him. And I think God speaks through the story of our lives, the things we already love, to guide us into the next chapter of the story—that is to say, to call us to do things we love in a way that blesses others and brings joy into our relationship with God.

So . . . what do you love?

Me? I love my children and my husband. I love Jesus. I don't always love them perfectly, but I'm willing to stick with it, to work on it.

I love the smoky, hazy smell of fall; I love snuggling with my kids in front of the fire on a winter afternoon; I love standing in my garden eating cherry tomatoes off the vine in summer; I love that deep breath-taking indigo of an early evening sky in spring.

I love books. Really a lot, I do. I'm one of the people Anne Lamott was talking about when she wrote:

> Because for some of us, books are as important as almost anything else on earth. What a miracle it is that out of these small, flat, rigid squares of paper unfolds world after world after world, worlds that sing to you, comfort and quiet or excite you. Books help us understand who we are and how we are to behave. They show us what community and friendship mean; they show us how to live and die.[1]

If you don't know what you love, think about your accomplishments. What do you feel proud of? What do you remember about your accomplishments as a child? Maybe you wrote a story or built a model or won a ribbon at the county fair. Maybe you had the winning project at a science fair or were a part of a winning team in basketball.

When I was in fifth grade, I set a goal of reading a hundred books (I told you I love books). I kept a list on purple notebook paper. I met that goal, and even though I didn't really tell very many people about it, it was an accomplishment that meant a lot to me. Looking back, that's just a little snapshot of what I am like as a person. It's a part of my story.

What would you guess former President Jimmy Carter would name as one of his greatest accomplishments? In 1984 Carter was in New York City and stopped by a Habitat for Humanity site where volunteers were renovating a six-story tenement in a rundown neighborhood. He offered to help, and eventually he and a group from Georgia returned to the project to work. "We slept in a church, and worked each day to help transform that old tenement into decent housing. It was dirty, sometimes dangerous work, but few accomplishments in life have given me greater satisfaction."[2]

This is a man who rubbed shoulders with world leaders and had held the highest office in the land. I'm sure he felt called to be the leader of the free world while he was in office. But after that experience, he decided to lend his name and influence to helping those who can't afford housing to have a roof over their heads. Doing that "grimy, sweaty work" and loving how it helped people gave him a sense of accomplishment, which led him to discover part of God's calling for this season of his life.

I want to consider these things, not just for the sake of self-awareness, which by itself can easily turn to self-absorption.

Rather, I ask myself who I am and what I love so that I can take it into the world and share something only I can give.

When I was a teenager, I organized a summer Bible study for some of the girls in my youth group. They were young women who had questions about the Bible. We'd sit on the front porch and read and discuss. No adult told me to do this or to set it up. God just opened the opportunity and I grabbed it. I didn't win an award for it, and sometimes not all the girls would show up. But it was an accomplishment just to have done it, and one way of listening to God is to reflect back on that part of my story. What does that tell me about God and about what he wants me to do?

Listening to that little chapter in my life's story, I realized that I love to teach. I love to discuss ideas. I didn't know what I would do with that at the time. Now, I did not become a famous Bible teacher. But I do teach and engage in conversation with people about spiritual things—through books, through leading studies or classes, through conversations with friends or my kids. It's part of what God has called me to do. I know that, in part, because of the experiences like that summer Bible study, of noticing what God gave me to do and how I felt doing it.

What is something you accomplished, even a small thing? What did you enjoy doing when you were younger? The answers to these questions—even the questions themselves—will tell you how to live your life.

I know that the life I ought to live includes books, and for me that has meant both reading and writing. It's where I find joy. That is, it's one of many places where I connect with God. When I read something profound or well written, it's like a worship experience. I just say, wow, God, thanks for giving these words and ideas to this writer. Thank you for bringing this book across my path, to help me see things more clearly or just think.

Sometimes I'll be at the computer, trying to figure out how to put words around the ideas that swirl in my brain, and the words will suddenly just come, and I'll just get them down, knowing God has given them to me. This doesn't always happen. It's when I show up and do the discipline of writing that sometimes God gives me ideas and words. I feel his smile at those moments, and I'm reassured that I'm doing what I should be doing, what he's called me to do. This makes me love God more—that he would be that good to me.

Being a parent and a gardener, being a writer and a friend—these are some of the ways I try to live into my identity as an image-bearer of a

> *If we consider the unblushing promises of reward and the staggering nature of the rewards promised in the Gospels, it would seem that Our Lord finds our desires, not too strong, but too weak. We are half-hearted creatures, fooling about with drink and sex and ambition when infinite joy is offered us, like an ignorant child who wants to go on making mud pies in a slum because he cannot imagine what is meant by the offer of a holiday at the sea. We are far too easily pleased.*
>
> —C. S. LEWIS[3]

supremely creative God. This is the life I am listening to. I have the privilege of being these things. So what am I going to do with that?

Sitting here writing with the window open, thinking about how to craft the words, showing up at my computer to write, even when I might want to be out just sitting in the garden—that's a creative expression that comes not just from my efforts but from my identity as someone created to continue creating. Knowing what I love will not tell me all the things I will do, but it will direct me toward a path.

∿ Listen to the Voice of Love ∿

As you think about what you love, what you are really trying to determine is where God gave you gifts. Joy is a gift. Accomplishments are a gift, a source of joy. They come as a result of our efforts joined with God's gifts to us.

We sometimes discount our accomplishments, or what we love. But these things matter. Not just to us. They matter to the people we will love and serve and help. Like the people Jimmy Carter and his teams build homes for. When we determine what we love, we see in it a way to love others and also see how we are loved.

God loves us enough to give us good gifts. When we ask, "What do I love?" we are really asking, "What good gifts has God given me?" For example, we may have people in our life—friends or family—that we love. They are a gift from God. We may love the beauty of nature—another gift. We may love doing certain things. Our ability to do them and do them well is a gift from God as well. By looking at what we love, we see where God is present in our lives. Those good gifts are his words to us. He is saying that he loves us enough to give generously to us. Through the things we love, he is calling us beloved.

Sometimes when I am teaching or serving with a team at church, I say, "I can't believe I get to do this. I get so much out of doing it." There's a paradox: I'm giving of my time, but I feel like I'm the one who receives. I'm doing something I love, something that God enables me to do, and through it, I express his love to others.

Henri Nouwen wrote:

> Every time you listen with great attentiveness to the voice
> that calls you the Beloved, you will discover within yourself
> a desire to hear that voice longer and more deeply. It is like

discovering a well in the desert. Once you have touched wet ground, you want to dig deeper.[4]

In order to listen to God, you have to know what he sounds like, to pick his voice out of the crowd. All day we think things, and people tell us things. Some of those thoughts, as well as words from others, come straight from God, and some don't. How can you tell which is which? Here's the thing: God always speaks with the voice of love. That doesn't mean that he always tells you what you want to hear. The voice that says, "Do the right thing," or, "It's going to be all right"—that's God. The voice that says, "You have screwed up again, so bad that you're unlovable"—that's not God's voice. He calls forth the best in us but not by condemning or shaming us. He does indeed call us beloved.

When have you known that you were God's beloved child? It may have been in a moment of quiet or when you were with a few people who know you well and love you in spite of that. It may have been in a moment when you were serving others in some way or creating something beautiful. Or when you felt lonely and afraid and then, somehow, you felt reassurance from God himself or from someone God put in your life to encourage you. Knowing that God loves us puts the story of our lives in a whole new light. No matter where you are on your spiritual journey, you've had encounters with God. But perhaps you did not recognize whose voice you were hearing.

That voice is there all the time, but sometimes it takes us a while to develop the ability to hear it. There are steps you can take, though, to tune in to it, to become aware of God and the voice that calls you beloved. I mean, sometimes we think God is just telling us what to do or what not to do. God does want to guide us, to have us make good choices. But he also wants us to know we are loved, because people who are loved make choices based on that. It seems to me that the good gifts he gives us remind us of that love. So I think we have to put ourselves in a place where we can receive those gifts.

Give yourself permission to live your life in a way that reflects who God made you to be. For example, if you are an introvert, make sure you schedule time to be alone. If you like to work with your hands, schedule time for doing that. It's not an indulgence. It's something that feeds your soul and allows you to listen.

I hear the voice of love very well when I am out of doors. God created me to love the outdoors—and gave me the gift of being a good observer. I see God's touch in every leaf, every bird, every flower. Gardening is experiential worship for me—noticing the miracle of growth, touching the earth. So I make it a spiritual practice to spend some time outdoors each day. It's part of listening to the voice of love. When I go for a walk in autumn and see a particularly brilliant tree, all decked out in red and gold, I think, wow, what a creative and amazing God! It feels like a gift from him to me. I feel like he's saying, I know you love beauty, so here's something special for you to enjoy. If someone does something like that for me, it makes me feel loved. So when I experience the joy of being in God's creation, to me it is a reminder that he loves me.

My husband loves sports. When he thinks about times of joy and accomplishment, especially from his childhood, those moments are often connected with sports—basketball, sailing, tennis. As a couple, we've learned that he is happier and saner and more joyful if he can spend time regularly playing tennis or sailing. I encourage him to take time for those things, because I know it brings him joy, and it is easier to live with him when he's happy! If we can engage in activities that bring us joy, we are reminded that God is good and generous and wants us to have joy, fun, freedom. And my husband finds he is more generous—he can give more to others—when he has been replenished by physical activity. He's also extroverted, so he loves doing sports with other people. It's part of how he extends God's love to others—to engage in fun activities with them.

Where have you felt joy? Do those things regularly. Are there people in your life who are positive and encouraging? Spend time with them; let them remind you that God is generous and kind. It's not always easy to remember that. Knowing your God is good and that you are the recipient of that goodness, that you are loved, even in the tough times, does take a bit of faith—faith enough to believe the voice of truth rather than the voice of doubt, the one that tells you that you are not good enough, that you couldn't possibly be worthy.

We sometimes think of faith as something we have or we don't. Many people can point to a time or a day when they put their faith in Jesus or decided they had enough faith that they could at least believe there was a God somewhere. But that's not the end of the story. Faith is something we need to get a little more of every day. We move on from "Yes, there is a God" to "God cares" to "God loves me personally and unconditionally." That's a journey, right there. And we take it a step at a time, asking for and receiving a little more faith, just enough each day. How do we do that? We have to "listen with great attentiveness to the voice that calls you the Beloved," as Nouwen said.

To get a little more faith each day, to get that day's manna, we have to show up. We have to find a quiet place to be still—to know that God is. We have to look for friendships where we are both affirmed and challenged. We have to show up at church, then serve and worship and participate—all things that build faith a little at a time. We have to show up in our family or our community and keep giving love to people who are not always easy to love. And be real enough with them to receive their love and encouragement, even if it's imperfect. We have to decide to act in a loving way.

God is writing the story of your life, but you are also shaping it, just by living it. You may not have noticed God, but that doesn't mean he hasn't been there. That's why I think it is so important to pay attention, not just to what has happened but what is happening, what choices you are making. By listening to your life, you can find God in the story. And sometimes we need to deliberately choose joy—choose to do and think and say things that will increase our joy—to take the gift God is offering us.

When we listen to and heed the voice of love, we join God in crafting the story, in doing the work that has been going on, and will go on. This voice does not always tell us what we want to hear, especially if we are heading in the wrong direction. But it always tells us the truth.

> *Joy is God's basic character. Joy is his eternal destiny. God is the happiest being in the universe. . . . As products of God's creation, creatures made in his image, we are to reflect God's fierce joy in life.*
>
> —JOHN ORTBERG[5]

We have to tune in to what the voice of love is saying. One way to do that is to simply notice where God has blessed you.

I recently realized that some of my family members (including me) were getting a little out of touch with their own belovedness. We all were being tempted to focus on what we didn't have, rather than what we did. We were listening more to fear than to love.

Sometimes a simple exercise can remind you of what is true. So we decided (actually, I decreed, if you must know) that we had to replace our negative thoughts with positive ones. So we began to keep a family journal. No secrets—we all can read it and write in it. We use it keep track of the blessings in our lives.

We call it our gratitude journal. At dinner together, we list five things we're grateful for in our day. One day in April we were grateful for the chives that had sprouted in the garden and the fact we could put them on the baked potatoes we had for dinner. We were also grateful that Scot had sold a house and that Melanie had a new bathing suit, which meant summer was coming. I don't edit the kids. If they want to be grateful for the dog or getting a haircut, that's fine. The important thing is to take time to notice. Keeping the journal makes us be intentional in a number of ways: about gathering for dinner, which is not easy during soccer season; about getting out the journal and coming up with a list of things we know are true; about checking our attitude. If we have a journal full of blessings, they can't all be accidents. Someone must love us. Being grateful is a way of listening, a way of noticing God in the story of your life. And that gratitude will lead us to joy.

∿ You Are Gifted ∿

If you listen, you will also hear God say, "You are gifted. I have given you gifts." Beyond the gifts of love and acceptance, God has given us spiritual gifts, which are abilities to serve or help or lead or encourage in a way that reflects the Giver and builds community with other people.

Our gifts enable us to extend our belovedness to others, to shepherd or encourage or show mercy to others. And if we listen to how God has gifted us and then actually use that gift to minister to others, we receive yet another gift: joy. You know that feeling, like hitting the ball on the sweet spot, knowing that this is what you were made to do and that God is smiling on the whole thing.

When I first started writing books on the spiritual life (which came as a surprise to everyone, including me, since I had been a newspaper reporter with a lot of doubts about my faith), a number of well-intentioned people (especially those at my publishing house who were trying desperately to figure out how to sell my books) began asking me, "Do you do any speaking?" I'd always been a writer, but I hadn't thought about having to have what marketing folks call a "platform"—a way to get your name out there by doing public speaking.

So I tried it. I had a friend who led a women's group at a small Methodist church near my home. I went and stood in the church basement and talked about the things I had written about. It was pretty awful. The spoken word didn't flow like the written one for me. I couldn't go back and revise a sentence like I could on paper. My voice also sounded as if someone were standing behind me, choking me.

Afterward, I was actually relieved. Now I could just tell people: no, I don't do speaking. I was fairly certain I did not have a gift for teaching. But for some reason, God opened a door for me to teach a class for women at my church. I laughed a little at God's very good sense of humor . . . But then I started to panic.

I sat down with my friend Debbie, who knows a lot about spiritual giftedness and who knew me fairly well, having been in a small group with me. I wanted to know what to do with these opportunities, since I obviously wasn't very good at teaching. I also knew that she was very direct and honest and wise, so she wouldn't pull any punches or tell me something just to try to make me feel good.

I told her that since I had been a small-group leader at church for years, I thought I was more of a shepherding person, not a teacher. I asked her what she thought I should do about these opportunities to teach. I wasn't a teacher, I was sure.

She pointed out that through my writing and by leading small groups, I had been teaching all along. "Keri, people who are shepherds are the type who walk alongside others and guide and encourage and get really excited about any itty-bitty small step of progress. They're very, *very* patient," she said. She paused and looked at me. "That's not you."

Great, I thought. I had been looking for honesty, but well, this was perhaps a bit more honest than I wanted. Not only was I bad at public speaking but, apparently, I was also seriously flawed in other ways! But Debbie, the wise woman, continued, "You want people to *get it*. You communicate really clearly when you're leading a discussion group or writing. That's teaching. Teachers want people to get it, to understand and apply things. You just need practice with the public speaking part of it, but teaching isn't the same as speaking. You've been teaching for years, just using a different method to communicate."

This, of course, terrified me. But sometimes God calls us to be braver than we think we can be. As I began to listen to what God was saying to me through this friend and through my life, as opportunities to speak kept coming my way, I realized I had a responsibility to the gift and the Giver to hone this gift, to use it and practice and get better. And here's the paradox: I began to enjoy it.

These days, I still prefer writing to speaking. And I still get evaluations that give sort of passive-aggressive, backhanded compliments about how I sound so much better in writing than when I'm speaking. Which I really have no problem with, honestly.

But I also get positive feedback. And regardless of the feedback, I feel pretty strongly that God has something to say through me, and I need to both speak and write, not so I can have a platform but because the voice of love needs me as one mouthpiece.

I write, yes, but I also teach with spoken words, whether it's in my home or a church basement or a retreat center. And I shake my head and wonder at how generous the Spirit is, giving gifts, because it brings me joy, and other people say it helps them. It's something I would never have experienced if I had listened only to my doubts rather than to the voice of love. Because I was willing to trust God to help me do what I could not do on my own, I've let a little of his light shine through.

How about you? Do you know what your spiritual gifts are? The Bible says each of us has at least one or two. Your gifts, your passions, your abilities—these are not just skills you've cultivated but things the Spirit has entrusted you with. Knowing what you love can often point you toward your passion and gifts, but sometimes you have to try things for a while before you realize that you love them. That means taking risks, trying things out, listening to the opportunities that come your way and to what other people say that they notice in you.

Talk to others and listen: What do they see in you as strengths? Read books on spiritual gifts; attend a seminar or class on this topic.

Maybe you've been given the gift of encouragement. Like all gifts, the only way to develop this gift is to use it. Encourage your family, and express your creativity with cards and notes to friends, kind words to your children. Shaping the souls of our children with encouragement and mercy and love—that's expressing the creativity within us as well.

Maybe you have a gift of leadership, and you're having trouble finding a place to exercise that gift. Searching it out is not only helpful; it is necessary. And two people who have the same gift, say of leadership, may be called to different things. One may be called to lead in the marketplace, another in a small group at church. But if you are a leader, you need to actually lead, to find a way to use that ability to honor God.

God has something for you to do with your life, and he's calling you to use what he's given you in a unique way to serve him and other people. What is that? That's what you have to figure out. Start asking yourself the big questions: What do I do well? What do others affirm in me? What makes me glad?

I remember first encountering the work of writer Frederick Buechner in my senior year of college—a time to listen to your life in an almost terrifying way as you prepare to make your way in the world, find a job, get a life, answer with your actions the questions you've theorized about for four years: What will I do, become, be? Because I was graduating from a Christian college, there was not just the "find a job" pressure but an underlying demand that we determine somehow whether the job we chose, whether it was missions or banking, was "God's will," as if that were something simple to determine, and whether we were doing something that God had gifted us and called us to do. We talked about calling, but really, we had no idea. Then I found Buechner.

"We must be careful with our lives, for Christ's sake, because it would seem that they are the only lives we are going to have in this puzzling and perilous world, and so they are very precious and what we do with them matters enormously," Buechner wrote in an essay titled "The Calling of Voices."[6] His words resonated with me but also felt weighty and pressured, as if God were saying, whatever you do, don't screw up. I tried to listen, but it made me nervous and afraid. I remember sitting in the student union reading those words to my fellow Lit and Philosophy majors and going, "Okay . . . How do we do this?"

So I was glad, as I read further in Buechner's essay:

> . . . Maybe that means that the voice we should listen to most as we choose a vocation is the voice that we might think we should listen to least, and that is the voice of our own gladness. What can we do that makes us gladdest, what can we do that leaves us with the strongest sense of sailing true north and of peace, which is much of what gladness is? Is it making things with our hands out of wood or stone or paint on canvas? Or is it making something we hope like truth out of words? Or is it making people laugh or weep in

a way that cleanses their spirit? I believe that if it is a thing that makes us truly glad, then it is a good thing and it is our thing and it is the calling voice that we were made to answer with our lives.[7]

Those words stirred my soul when I was twenty-two years old and embarking on a career. And they still do. I knew that "making something we hope like truth out of words" was one thing I could do, and loved to do, and wanted always to do, and was in fact what I had been doing for most of my life already. It was what gave me the "strongest sense of sailing true north."

But listening to the voice of your own gladness is sometimes hard. Sometimes I don't feel glad, and to try to manufacture it feels shatteringly naïve. It's also hard to hear and pay attention to your own gladness, your own heart, when critics speak louder: if you must be a writer, why don't you do the type of writing that actually pays well?

My inner critic has cousins, who may live in your heart, too. They might say things like: Why waste your college education staying home with your children? Your job is boring and mundane and couldn't possibly make a difference to anyone. You may be happy and successful now, but pretty soon the other shoe is going to drop.

What gives you the strongest sense of sailing true north and of peace? It may be the thing you do for a career, and it may not. That's okay. But if you don't think you've ever felt that—well, maybe this book can help.

For me, if I do not write, I put my light under a bushel, or snuff it out, or at least plug up the place where truth wanted to flow out from God's abundant supply to this place and time.

The universe will simply go on surging, looking for someone willing to turn on the switch and put the lamp on a stand—someone, possibly, who has much and will be given more, because they were willing to listen and to receive it!

Read, research, ask, listen. Try serving in different areas in your community, in your church. Find out how God has gifted you by trying different things. Investigating by simply doing things is a key part of listening to your life. I think if people figure out what gift God put in them, and then they use it, they help the voice of love shout a little louder in this world. And God knows, we all need that.

∿ Listen for the Light ∿

I think Jesus knows how easy it is for us to miss things, to simply not pay attention and not hear what he wants to tell us. That may be one of the many reasons he told people, "Consider carefully how you listen." Wise counsel, of course. But look at the context of this comment:

> No one lights a lamp and hides it in a jar or puts it under a bed. Instead, he puts it on a stand, so that those who come in can see the light. For there is nothing hidden that will not be disclosed, and nothing concealed that will not be known or brought out into the open. Therefore consider carefully how you listen. Whoever has will be given more; whoever does not have, even what he thinks he has will be taken from him [Luke 8:16–18].

Until I was writing this book on listening, I never noticed Jesus' comment in this passage. Growing up evangelical, I sang "This little light of mine, I'm gonna let it shine." This, as we all know, means witnessing, telling others about Jesus and the four spiritual laws and how to get saved. I figured my light wasn't very bright since I did that only very rarely, and when I did I usually became lightheaded and felt I would faint. Anyway, listening had very little to do with it. Besides, why was that sentence about listening in there anyway? Jesus seems to be mixing metaphors. He's talking about light and seeing and then, suddenly, about listening?

Jesus does that a lot. He pays no attention to the conventions of storytelling; he mixes metaphors right and left; he talks in riddles and word-pictures that, he readily admits, confound the wise. The thing is, though, Jesus always speaks with the voice of love.

How can a word—something we hear—be a light—something we see? It's the mixing of these metaphors that makes us think. By hearing and listening we become "enlightened." We just get it a little better than we did before.

It seems that Jesus especially loves to play with this idea of "light." Of course, it's not just a thing that we see but what makes understanding possible. He says, "consider carefully how you listen," right after talking about light, because words give us light or, in other words, understanding.

The Bible says, "Your word is a lamp to my feet and a light for my path" (Psalm 119:105). A little later in the same psalm, we see this truth: "The entrance of your words gives light, it gives understanding to the simple" (verse 130).

And if we think we've got it all figured out, and we don't need any more information, any more listening, think again: "even what he thinks he has will be taken from him."

So we have to let the light shine, because the fact is, the light is there. If we don't listen and let it shine through us, it will shine through someone else. God will find a way. The Bible says, "The eyes of the Lord range throughout the earth, to strengthen those whose hearts are fully committed to him" (2 Chronicles 15:9). Another version puts it, "that he may strongly support those whose hearts are fully his."

In other words, the Spirit is flowing, moving, looking for someone to flow through. Jesus is the light of the world, and he wants to live in us, shine through us. We can join in, or we can stand by and let someone else step up. But if we're invited to dance, why wouldn't we?

Letting God's light flow through your life does not mean you will end up on the mission field or becoming a pastor. It may mean deciding that you are going to take a certain job, even if it doesn't seem to "advance" your career, so that you can spend more time with your family.

A few years ago, I wrote an article for the local newspaper about a woman from my church who went on a week-long mission trip to an orphanage in Mexico. She met many children, but one little boy in particular stole her heart. His name was Marco, and he adorable, but he was very sick. And in this part of the Baja of Mexico, the brain surgery he needed (a fairly common surgery in the United States) was not available. The missionaries at the orphanage said the child would die soon, and there was nothing that could be done. It happened all the time, and it was sad, but, unfortunately, not that unusual. The woman wished there was something she could do for Marco and his family, who lived on the $1 a day or so that his mother earned picking tomatoes.

Through a rather amazing series of events, a nurse who was also on the trip found a neurosurgeon at the hospital where she worked who agreed to do the work pro bono. The woman was able to fly Marco up to Chicago for surgery, then she kept Marco in her home for about two months to recover, then brought him back to Mexico.

Some of her well-meaning friends told her she was crazy, but she said she felt God was telling her to help this one child. The way things fell into place told her she had to keep dancing, to keep going. She said the verse that kept coming to mind was, "Do not withhold good from those who deserve it, when it is in your power to act" (Proverbs 3:27).

So the woman listened to God, and then God's light shone through her and a few of her friends. She still keeps in touch with Marco's family, tries to help when she can. She's tried to help them find better housing, better care for Marco. They are still poor; they have challenges she can hardly fathom beyond Marco's health. But she listened to what God asked her to do and then did it. Beyond what she did for the family, she says, her life has changed. Listening and acting took her story in a whole new direction, taught her about listening to God, and her life will never be the same.

If I have just a little faith, generated simply by inviting the voice of love into a debate with the voice of doubt, daring to host a dialogue in the dark room of my soul, that act of courage alone generates enough light—or at least provides an outlet for God to shine—so that everyone can see a little better. But I have to choose to listen more closely, to trust the voice of love, even when doubt and fear shout and cuss. The voice of love calls me to make choices that are right but amazingly difficult. Listening to love is an act of trust. And when we trust, we get better at it. Our faith grows, and we can hear God more clearly. Which is why you and I are having the conversation of this book in the first place, isn't it?

 What sort of things do you "fool about" with, thinking they will bring you joy? What do you think Lewis meant when he said that we are "too easily pleased"?

Sit for one minute and list things that you could do to reflect God's joy, to bring joy into your life. You might include anything from taking bubble baths, to playing with kids, to reading a great book, to eating more chocolate. Don't edit yourself; don't try to sound "religious" or even "deep." Just brainstorm. Pick one or two of the items on your list, and do them today.

CHAPTER II

How Have I Struggled?

Why are you downcast, O my soul?
Why so disturbed within me?

—PSALM 42:5

The first time it happened, I laughed. A bit nervously. But after a while, I began to wonder: Was there something wrong with me?

I'd find myself driving the carpool and, after dropping the kids off at a practice or lesson, as I drove over the interstate highway that cuts through the middle of the suburb we live in, I'd look longingly at the cars streaming toward Rockford. I'd think, briefly but fiercely: Do I really have to go home and start dinner? I could just hop on the highway and head west. I could just keep driving.

I suspect I am not the only one who finds herself thinking like this. Irrational thoughts are actually pretty normal for most of us. But I was aware that something was going on. For the last few years, I've been doing ministry and writing, but sometimes I wrestle with doubt. I think my desire to escape is not just about stress but about the doubts I sometimes find myself facing. I teach and write on spiritual life, but I would sometimes ask myself: Am I living the life I'm inviting others to explore? Who am I to write and speak on the spiritual life? More importantly, is the life I'm inviting others into really a wise path?

Most good theologians will tell you that doubt is good. It is the whetstone that sharpens our faith, helps us to really ask and understand why we believe what we do. Some say it purifies belief, strengthens it.

Still, when you start having escape fantasies, even ones your rational mind tells you are ridiculous and impossible, ones that make your conscience laugh uncomfortably and ask, Now, where did *that* come from?—that is something to pay attention to. So I did. What's up with that? I wondered. Why would a middle-aged mom with what appeared to be a very normal life—some stresses, some joys, just normal—why would she fantasize, even if only for an irrational moment or two, about driving her minivan off into the sunset and not looking back?

Don't misunderstand: I am crazy about my kids, my husband. I'm deeply committed to my family and our little place in the world. We're part of an imperfect but really amazing church. I love the neighborhood where we live. It oozes with families we enjoy being with—even the dog has buddies down the street. I'm able to do work that I love, even if I question it sometimes. We have a good life here. So when the doubts came knocking, I'd peer out the peephole at them, shake my head and say, What are you, nuts?

Struggle is part of the human experience. M. Scott Peck said it best in the opening lines of his classic book, *The Road Less Traveled*. He writes:

Life is difficult. This is a great truth, one of the greatest truths. It is a great truth because once we truly see this truth, we transcend it. Once we truly know that life is difficult— once we truly understand and accept it—then life is no longer difficult. Because once it is accepted, the fact that life is difficult no longer matters.[1]

Struggle comes in countless forms and circumstances. Some people, it seems, have a life with a higher challenge factor than others. Perhaps illness, a wayward child, disappointments in relationships, or lack thereof, have created difficulties that seem at times overwhelming. Others find that certain seasons of life have more struggles than others—that things will go along smoothly for a while and then you hit a bump or two in the road.

The Bible never promises that a life of faith is an easy one. It does tell us, though, that God comforts us when we struggle. Look how the Apostle Paul opens his letter to the church at Corinth:

> Praise be to the God and Father of our Lord Jesus Christ, the Father of compassion and the God of all comfort, who comforts us in all our troubles, so that we can comfort those in any trouble with the comfort we ourselves have received from God [2 Corinthians 1:3–4].

Notice it does not say, "Praise God that we don't have any troubles."

Later in the same book, Paul writes: "We are hard pressed on every side, but not crushed; perplexed, but not in despair; persecuted, but not abandoned; struck down, but not destroyed" (2 Corinthians 4:8–9).

I'm not trying to be negative. I just want to point out that part of life is the struggle of it, which sometimes makes us doubt, which seems to add to the struggle. But I believe that if we listen to our struggles, they will actually lead us, not to doubt but to God (although we may have to take a little detour through doubt before we get there). It's a process that takes time, but listening can transform our struggles, and our struggles can transform our listening.

While I don't want to focus on my struggles, I think they have lessons in them—things that can help me notice God in my life. The struggles are part of the story. As Frederick Buechner writes, "Whenever you find tears in your eyes, especially unexpected tears, it is well to pay the closest attention."[2] Even if your life's challenges don't always bring you to tears, it is still important to pay attention—that is, to listen.

The escape thing was just one sign of my restlessness. I was questioning everything, it seemed. It felt very much like a cliché to call it a midlife crisis, but I was a month from my forty-second birthday, so call it what you'd like.

> *You have to live through your pain gradually and thus deprive it of its power over you. . . . What is your pain? It is the experience of not receiving what you most need. It is a place of emptiness where you feel sharply the absence of the love you most desire. . . . You have to begin to trust that your experience of emptiness is not the final experience, that beyond it is a place where you are being held in love.*
>
> —HENRI NOUWEN[3]

It had been building for months, perhaps even a few years—a subterranean restlessness born out of resistance to God's calling on my life. Part of it was just a fear that I was unable to do what God had called me to, or at least unable to do it as well as I had hoped, or that what I was doing contained any meaning or significance at all.

When I spoke to God about my doubts, my fear, my unrest, I got nothing except direction to keep listening—that is, to listen to the story of my life so far, and to wrestle with the doubts and questions that seemed to be the focus lately, and to say, "What do you want me to learn, God?"

"Listen to your heart," the Spirit seemed to say. "Don't listen for easy answers but for the mystery. Just wait and trust." To be okay with unresolved issues is not easy for me.

God seemed to be saying, Are you spending as much time just being *with* me as you are doing stuff *for* me? How often do you get quiet and just rest? I felt like Jesus was inviting me to just be still, to admit that yes, life was sometimes difficult. In the midst of it, he invited me to listen to the voice of love—by being quiet, by believing that I didn't have to work so hard to earn anyone's approval, especially God's. And to notice that, wow, I was doing a lot and actually getting kind of tired. I wanted to just be still. It sounded good. But the voice of doubt seemed to want to pick a fight, or at least to argue loudly.

I'd been on this journey a while—several years, actually. I had begun to listen to what I was reading, thinking, journaling. I was pretty sure I was on a path to growth—moving away from living a faith governed by rules and toward a more honest relationship with Jesus, one in which I could be myself, one that was not based on performance or perfection but freedom to be who I really was. I felt I was moving forward into what God had called me to do and be. But I'd found that, despite the growth, I felt uncertain. My doubts had been lurking in the background, but now they were getting just a little more insistent. I found myself wondering at times what I really did believe, and why.

Sue Monk Kidd writes candidly about her own midlife experience in her book *When the Heart Waits*. What she realized was that she needed to wait on God, to receive grace in God's timing, not her own. She says this:

> Crisis, change, all the myriad upheavals that blister the spirit
> and leave us groping—they aren't voices simply of pain but
> also of creativity. And if *we would only listen* [italics mine],
> we might hear such times beckoning us to a season of wait-
> ing, to the place of fertile emptiness.[4]

Despite reading Kidd's book and resonating with it, I still was impatient to get my life figured out, to dispense with my doubts as efficiently as possible. I didn't really want to have a "season of waiting." I wanted to get things figured out, settled, resolved. But her words encouraged me to listen, to embrace my restless questions of faith and identity: Who was I? What did I believe? Was the vocation I was throwing myself into the thing I was really supposed to be doing? My calling was strongly affirmed by some people. But others did not offer me that same affirmation. And I realized that I really wanted affirmation.

I wanted other people's approval, especially certain people—not just tacit or grudging approval but their wildly effusive admiration. I wanted to know that I was good enough, that I was okay. While we all want to be loved and approved of, I was letting this come between me and people I loved.

I know the Bible says we're to listen to God, even when other people don't seem that supportive. In fact, Jesus said, "Blessed are you when people insult you, persecute you and falsely say all kinds of evil against you because of me. Rejoice and be glad, because great is your reward in heaven, for in the same way they persecuted the prophets who were before you" (Matthew 5:11–12).

Such words do not always comfort. I wanted encouragement and felt like I did not get enough of it. I was disappointed. It raised doubts about what I was doing, and if I was doing ministry, was I doing it for the right reasons?

It's possible that the voice of doubt had been there all along, but I had been able to ignore it for a long time. When I stopped ignoring, started listening, I was forced to slow down. Or maybe the slowing came first. But moving at a slower pace made it impossible to ignore the questions that I'd been skimming over, like a bird flying just above the surface of the water. Now it was as if I were diving, thinking I saw the flash of a fish in that same water. Would I come up with anything?

Maybe I just needed to listen, and then the doubts would go away. Well, that sounds nice, but I realize now it doesn't work that way. As I moved toward just simply being with God (instead of doing stuff *for* God), I thought life would somehow get easier. I'd hoped to hear nothing but joyful affirmations, but, unfortunately, God sometimes speaks through the questions.

Another part of my angst at the time had to do with the fact that it sort of dawned on me that after fourteen years of marriage, my husband Scot and I still had to work at it—at making life together work, at deciding each day to love each other when it was hard and there were stress and bills and busyness, at choosing to forgive each other again and again. And it was dawning on me that we'd have to keep doing that—forging our relationship. We'd make progress, yes, but also there were times we disappointed each other. I wanted it to be easier; I'd hoped by this point we might be able to coast a bit. Not that it was all hard work. We had many times of laughter, of just fun and joy and playfulness. But also, because we both wanted a strong relationship, there was effort required. Sometimes, this made me feel weary. And I knew I needed to listen to that weariness, because I had created some of it myself by being so determined to make everyone happy.

I fooled myself into thinking I had hidden my people-pleasing tendencies. I was pretty sure people thought of me as a strong, independent person, with a deep commitment to my faith and my family. I thought of myself that way, frankly.

I was learning that I needed to listen to my life. I wanted to pay attention in an even deeper way—to listen not only to my accomplishments and creative expression but also to my pain and struggles. For years I had been reading, studying, writing, and even teaching people about how to listen to God, how to open themselves up to God and grow spiritually. And yet it was my doubts that pushed me to an even deeper place. God was trying to speak to me through my life, through the doubts and questions embedded in it.

As I began to embrace my doubts and struggles, I happened to talk to Debbie again—my friend who had so bluntly told me I was not a shepherd. I told her some of my frustrations. I was hoping she would reinforce my notion that it is just so hard to be me. No such luck. She challenged me to think about how I enable people to treat me the way I do, to own up to the choices I make, the boundaries I had unwittingly refused to set. To stop looking to Scot, my parents, my closest friends, or anyone else for things that, really, only God could give me. I was not very happy to hear this; in fact, I think I ended the conversation rather quickly and spent some time crying and feeling sorry for myself.

But after I'd spent my tears, I listened. Was there any truth in what she'd said? Was it possible that God was speaking through her loving but direct words? Was it possible that my trying to make everyone happy was making me miserable? What if I listened when people tried to blame or manipulate and then said, "No, I'm not going to take that on. I'm not going to allow you to treat me that way." What would happen if I worked hard to listen to what people were really saying and to how I reacted? When people were unhappy, did I try to fix them? What would happen if I just quit doing that? What if I learned to set boundaries instead of working so hard on things I couldn't really control anyway?

∿ Living the Questions ∿

I am not uncomfortable with questions. Before having kids, I was a reporter for a large newspaper. I asked questions for a living. But reporters ask questions and get answers. Even when someone would say, "No comment," I'd ask another question, or the same question, subtly rephrased, until I received an answer. I remember interviewing a particularly belligerent politician when I was a rookie reporter. I kept after him, baiting him with lawyerly questions ("Isn't it true . . . ?" and "Your political rivals are saying . . .")

until his frequent "no comment's" melted into answers that gave me a scoop for the next morning's paper.

Who? What? Where? Why? When? How? That was what I asked. It's what every reporter is trained to ask. If I didn't get answers, my editor would send me back to call one more source, track down another fact or a quote to give my readers as much information as I could.

But in faith and life, questions do not always have such easy answers, perhaps because the questions themselves are a little more complicated than Who? What? and Where?

As I began to try to figure out how to listen to my life, I encountered this bit of wisdom from poet Rainer Maria Rilke:

> I beg you . . . to be patient toward all that is unsolved in your heart and to try to love *the questions themselves* like locked rooms and like books that are written in a very foreign tongue. Do not now seek the answers, which cannot be given you because you would not be able to live them. And the point is, to live everything. *Live* the questions now. Perhaps you will then gradually, without noticing it, live along some distant day into the answer.[5]

"Live the questions"? "Love the questions"? What does that mean? Live everything? What would that look like? I loved questions—but only those I could track down answers for. In my soul I knew these ideas had been simmering a long time. Rilke's quote only put those vague stirrings into lovely, heart-piercing prose. I wanted to be present, to show up and be there when the voice of love and the voice of my doubts sat down to debate.

As a former reporter, living with ambiguity, with unanswered questions—that was not easy. But it had to be better than what I had been doing thus far; even if I didn't fully understand it, I knew I had to move down this path.

One of the questions that God brought into my life was simply this: How are you feeling? I thought I was in touch with my feelings. I realized one night that I had far to go.

Scot and I decided we would sign up for a marriage seminar at church—for a little assistance, you know. This wasn't one of those quick weekend deals. No, this was scheduled for a number of weeks in a row.

So the first night we sat around a table in the church gym with other couples. We had just heard a lecture on how our marriage issues stem from core fears: the fear under everything else—like fear of abandonment or fear that we are not loved. To oversimplify it, we're often motivated by fear. Like when your husband gets mad at you for overspending and you get defensive about it, his core fear is that you won't have enough and your core fear is that he really doesn't love you. And you had to name the fear in order to realize that the surface issue is really not what you are arguing about. And then you can reassure each other: there *will* be enough; he *does* love you.

I tried to listen, but I held my heart carefully, protecting it, trying to be rational, logical, anything but emotional. Hmmm, isn't that interesting? I'd say to myself as I listened to the speaker.

When the lecture was done, we had to go around the table and just "check in" to start our discussion group time. We started by simply having each person answer the question: How are you feeling?

How are you feeling? The question seemed innocent enough. To help the men (and others of us who seemed to be in denial), there was a chart with words to choose from: Sad, Angry, Scared, Happy, Excited, Tender.

Everyone said things like, "Happy to be here." One person admitted being a little scared about having to work on her marriage. When it was my turn, I stared at the list of words. To my shock and embarrassment, I started crying. "How am I feeling? I'm angry and sad and disappointed and, and, and . . ."

Suddenly, I was also embarrassed. I didn't really know these people, and I didn't want to be here, at a marriage seminar, with everyone looking at me with sympathy and a bit of shock.

"I'm sorry," I said. I got up and walked over to the water cooler, filled the plastic cup with water and stood there drinking it, trying to breathe. I wanted to leave. But I knew I had to live the questions, much as everything down to the bottom of me wanted to bolt. Slowly, I turned and walked back to the table.

In the weeks that followed, I kept going back to that stupid seminar, learning how to dialogue and listen, and getting very angry about the fact that Scot and I didn't dialogue or listen to each other very well, or at least the way I imagined that all the other people around our table did. Thankfully, the other couples became a bit more honest as time went on. Still, I was sad and angry that my marriage was not always easy. And that most marriages are difficult, at least sometimes. I realized that my husband truly loved me, but he was never going to be able to do it perfectly. Because people can't. They don't love you perfectly. But it was freeing to realize this, to let go of my unreasonable expectations, and say, okay, who can love me? And I sensed God, not speaking, but sort of raising his hand and catching my eye, like someone bidding at an auction.

I had to face the fact that some of the pain was actually inside of me and had been there long before I ever met my husband, that life had wounded me way before I met Scot, and some of those wounds were inevitable and some were the result of my own bad choices. I had to take responsibility for my own junk. And as much as I loved Scot, I often let fear get in the way.

This did not resolve things right away. It was—and is—still a struggle. A few months later, I spoke to a friend of mine about the pain in my heart—and those irrational impulses to try to escape. She told me about a time she was in great pain. She remembered a day she walked for hours, but she couldn't get away from the pain. "It goes with you, no matter where you go. You can't run from it. You have to face it," she told me.

Darn. I had been secretly hoping that perhaps I could somehow change my circumstances—get my husband and children and friends and parents to somehow morph into something else—and that would alleviate those fears that caused me pain.

 If we can't discern the Lord's voice in our life, we will be at the beck and call of every other voice. The voice of shame, perhaps, from some failure in our past. . . . If we have heard from the Savior's own lips how much he loves us and delights in us, it will silence the taunt of voices that put a makeup mirror to our face and point out all the reasons why Jesus couldn't possibly be in love with such a blemished person.

—KEN GIRE[6]

Nope. I had to listen to my pain and struggles. I had to do some hard work at looking at my past mistakes, at my upbringing, at my life. I had to listen to the pain and struggles of my life in order to heal it.

The two voices we talked about earlier are both trying to address the pain in our lives. The voice of love says: God is with you; you can endure. And the voice of fear says: give up, run away or tune out, distance yourself emotionally from the person or thing that you think is causing you pain. But as my friend pointed out, the pain goes with you. And if you do live this "looks great outside, dying inside" dualism, you'll give the voice of fear the foothold, because it will become the voice of shame and will start talking louder.

So that's what I'm working on. It stinks; it's not fun. But I am learning that if I ignore my pain, it will fester and never heal. The good news is, if you listen to your struggles, you will begin to know where you need to heal and, ultimately, where you can provide healing to a hurting world.

Listening to Pain

Many people, if you ask them to tell you about a time when they experienced great personal growth, will point to a time of struggle or difficulty. Why is that?

If we are to really listen to our lives, we have to ask: Where have I struggled? It will give us insight into what our lives are about. Our pain and our doubts reveal much about us, and the events and people that shaped us.

Sometimes we struggle because there is something we need to change. Perhaps we need to let go of negative patterns of behavior. Other times, we find resistance and struggle when we try to do what is right, and we must continue to soldier on, trusting him to rescue us, to deliver us.

God whispers to us in our pleasures, speaks in our conscience, but shouts in our pain: it is His megaphone to rouse a deaf world.

—C. S. LEWIS[7]

Throughout the Bible, God is called a rescuer, a deliverer, a helper in times of trouble. When you struggle, when you are disappointed, you can listen to what God wants to say to you: "The Lord is close to the brokenhearted and saves those who are crushed in spirit" (Psalm 34:18).

The other night I was at church. One of our former pastors, John Ortberg, was there and gave a great message about hope that went beyond just being positive or optimistic. He based his message on the passage from 2 Corinthians that talks about how we are "hard pressed on every side, but not crushed"—verses 8 through 10, which I quoted earlier in this chapter. The passage ends with this exhortation:

> Therefore, we do not lose heart. Though outwardly we are
> wasting away, yet inwardly we are being renewed day by day.
> For our light and momentary troubles are achieving for us
> an eternal glory that far outweighs them all. So we fix our
> eyes not on what is seen, but what is unseen.

The message was about how even things that seem not to be "light and momentary troubles" are actually just that, because what matters is our heart, our eternity. I was moved and encouraged, but God had more to tell me.

I was in the bookstore after the service when someone called my name. I looked up to see a small woman smiling at me. She did not look very well, actually, except that she was beaming at me with what I can only call an unusual joy. She was sporting a very short crew cut, through which you could see a large scar that wound laterally across her somewhat bumpy scalp. Her skin looked dry and fragile, her eyes, though bright, looked tired. What little hair she had was peppered with gray.

We had served together at the church, she as a designer, I as a volunteer writer. I hadn't seen her for probably nine or ten years. "Lisa, how are you?" I said, trying unsuccessfully to keep my eyes from drifting toward her battered scalp. She's a head shorter than me, which made this impossible.

"Well, I'm a survivor," she said. "Yes," I said, waiting, listening—a little afraid of what I was going to hear but knowing at the same time God wanted me to hear it.

"I just recently had to have brain surgery to remove a tennis-ball-sized tumor," she said. But the expression in her voice didn't match it. It was like she was telling me she had won the lottery. She smiled at me.

"Oh, I'm so sorry," I began.

"No, don't be," she said. She went on to describe a near-death experience during the surgery, complete with angelic choirs singing in the background, a white room with a door and light coming from under the door, and God telling her, no, don't go through the door, it's not yet your time, I have things for you to do.

"If he would have told me to, I would have opened the door and gone," she said. "The pull was that strong."

The experience happened twice during her stay in the hospital, even though she had surgery only once. After the first time, she was alive but groggy. When she awakened the second time, she was thinking clearly and appeared to be fully recovered.

She would have left five children under the age of eight if God had told her to open the door. She held her youngest in her arms, a tiny, wide-eyed child. Her husband came up. He took the petite little girl from Lisa, holding her in his arms. "They told us she would never walk," he said, and I realized now he was talking about the baby. He set her on the floor with a flourish, where she clung to his pant leg for a moment, lurched a bit, then began to toddle away. "They said she wouldn't live more than eight days, that she was going to die," he said. "But look—they were wrong!" He scooped up the child and held her to his cheek. The look of triumph and joy on both their faces was amazing. And disconcerting. This made no sense. They'd been through hell. They had heard the voice of fear, and now they were able to laugh at it. Because the voice of love was stronger. Their youngest child, this tiny little girl, had pneumonia as a newborn and wasn't supposed to survive. But she did. Lisa had a tumor the size of her fist in her brain, and God had healed her.

"If anyone needs a miracle, tell them to talk to us," they told me, certain that the power of God was strong in their lives. "We'll pray for them." And I thought, outwardly, we are wasting away. But inwardly, we are being renewed.

We can be happy because of our circumstances, but true joy comes in spite of them.

I know I've felt overwhelmed simply having two kids and a busy life. Here was a woman with five children, averaging eighteen months apart each, surviving brain cancer and almost losing the last baby. She didn't seem overwhelmed, except perhaps with a joy I could not even comprehend. It was like God sent me a little illustration for the sermon I had just heard, asking me, Were you listening there? Your troubles really are light and momentary. What matters is the heart. Focus there.

Where have you struggled? Maybe someone you love has had cancer but didn't get to have that miraculous recovery. Maybe someone you loved died young, died violently, or abandoned you.

> *The closest communion with God comes, I believe, through the sacrament of tears. Just as grapes are crushed to make wine and grain to make bread, so the elements of this sacrament come from the crushing experiences of life.*
>
> —KEN GIRE[8]

Maybe you have struggled with infertility, and you don't understand why God has not given you what you want most of all, and why every time you see a pregnant woman or a person pushing a stroller or you have to go to someone's baby shower, it's like you're swallowing broken glass.

Maybe you're in a difficult marriage or you wrestle with depression. Maybe your pain is just the dull ache of boredom, because you think your life is mostly safe but not very exciting. Sometimes we want to run from the pain, but I think there are lessons in it. Not neat and tidy sitcom-type solutions but connections that we can make with God, with truth.

In order to make those connections, we have to invite God into the pain.

One of the ways we listen to our lives is simply to notice where we are and what things have happened to us, not necessarily what God has even done to us. Somehow, I have ended up where I am, whether by God's intervention or my own choices, or other people's choices, or a blend of those things.

Instead of complaining about where you are, notice it and say, "How did I get here? What can change and what can't? What about my life does God want to redeem? What does he want to accomplish in me, and in others, through my life's pain and challenges?"

The last thirteen chapters of the book of Genesis in the Bible tell the story of Jacob's family, focusing on his son Joseph, who is sold into slavery by his jealous brothers. Joseph faces difficulties and struggles through his life. He's sold into slavery, falsely accused of adultery, put into prison. But the story repeatedly tells us "the Lord was with him," and so in time he becomes the ruler of Egypt, second only to the Pharaoh in power.

Eventually, he is reunited with his brothers and even his father, who had thought he was dead. At the end of the story, even though Joseph has repeatedly shown them kindness, the brothers seem unable to accept his forgiveness. They are still more than a little embarrassed by how they treated Joseph way back when and fearful of what will happen, as you can see from the text:

> His brothers then came and threw themselves down before him. "We are your slaves," they said. But Joseph said to them, "Don't be afraid. Am I in the place of God? You intended to harm me, but God intended it for good to

accomplish what is now being done, the saving of many lives. So then, don't be afraid" [Genesis 50:18–21].

There may have been people in your life who intended to harm you or did so without even realizing it. God didn't bring that pain, but he can take those struggles, that pain, and use it for good to help others—or just to help you.

As I have wrestled with forging a better marriage, with the challenges of parenting, with my career, with friendships that haven't gone the way I expected, I sometimes have trouble finding God in the story of my life.

But God offers to meet us when we feel disturbed or sad. Our struggles may lead us to doubt for a while, but ultimately, I think my doubts have sharpened my faith, made it tougher and more real. To even ask the questions means I think there must be an answer, or a purpose. There must be hope. The Bible affirms this. Look at the context of the psalm I quoted at the opening of this chapter:

> *Why are you downcast, O my soul?*
> *Why so disturbed within me?*
> *Put your hope in God,*
> *For I will yet praise him,*
> *My Savior and my God.*
> *My soul is downcast within me;*
> *Therefore I will remember you*
> —PSALM 42:5–6

Listen to your struggles, but then listen to the voice of love that speaks through those struggles. Remind yourself—*remember* what God has done: sought you out and loved you, no matter what. Listen to his voice. That voice will tell you about who you are and how you can love others. Your struggles are unique, but they also connect you to other people and give you a platform from which to shout out the voice of love to others.

 Talk about a time when you felt an absence of the love you most desired. What is it like to experience emptiness? What do you think Nouwen meant by saying there is a place beyond the emptiness?

Do you ever find yourself "at the beck and call of every other voice" but God's? What would you need to do to be able to hear from Jesus how much he loves you and delights in you?

If Lewis is right, then God is always communicating. Do you agree that God "shouts in our pain"? Do you draw closer to God in times of struggle? Have painful or difficult circumstances been a catalyst for growth in your life?

Was there a time when your tears brought you close to God? What have the "crushing experiences of life" produced in your soul?

CHAPTER III

What Is My Desire?

In the children's story *Miss Rumphius,* the title character is an eccentric, kind old aunt we all wish we had. She grows up beside the sea with her grandfather, who tells her stories of the faraway places he has visited.

She resolves that when she grows up, she too will visit far-away places and then return to live by the sea when she is old. "That is all very well," her grandfather tells her. "But there is one more thing that you must do. You must do something to make the world more beautiful."

Miss Rumphius grows up and travels the world, seeing wonders and having all sorts of adventures, but eventually hurts her back while camel-riding and must simply go home and rest. She loves flowers, so she plants a few seeds in the stony ground outside her little cottage by the sea. By the next spring, she cannot do much because her back is bothering her. She notices that the seeds she planted have sprouted into purple, blue, and rose-colored lupines outside her window.

"I have always loved lupines best," she says. "I wish I could plant more seeds." But she is too weak and unwell.

By the following spring, she has recovered her strength. She goes for a walk and is amazed to see that when she walks over the hill behind her house, the wind and birds have spread the seeds from her garden, and lupines are now growing there, too.

It is then that Miss Rumphius knows what to do to make the world more beautiful. She goes home and orders five bushels of lupine seeds and spends her summer walking highways and lanes, sowing lupines.

People call her the crazy lupine lady. But the next spring, there are lupines everywhere. And she continued this for several years—sowing lupine seeds, making her little corner of the world a bit more beautiful.

When Miss Rumphius tells her niece Alice, the narrator of the story, that she, too, must do something to make the world more beautiful, Alice tells us: "'Alright,' I say. But I do not know yet what that can be."[1]

Miss Rumphius had a desire—to see the world, to live beside the sea, and, finally, to make the world a little more beautiful. She knew what she loved: beauty, especially lupine flowers. She had her struggles—getting older, a bad back that kept her in bed for a year. Certainly, she was living the questions, especially the one about what she could do to make the world more beautiful. And she listened to her life. She listened to the stories her grandfather told her; she listened to the people she met on her journeys, and she listened to that key question: What can I do to make the world more beautiful? It was that question, and the way the lupines spread, even without her help, that gave her a vision for how to live her life.

The story stirs something in us—a desire for meaning and significance, a desire to, like Miss Rumphius, do something to make the world more beautiful. For many of us, Alice's words resonate: I do not know yet what that can be. But we long, somewhere deep inside, to find out.

Sometimes, making the world more beautiful, living in God's story, happens with just small acts of listening and obeying God's voice.

I had an opportunity to do just that recently. I was in Denver, Colorado, for a convention of Christian publishers and retailers. I stayed right in the heart of the city. During the day, I had meetings with publishers, editors, marketing people, other authors. But each morning, I took a long walk and then had time to sit in a sidewalk café, writing and people watching, drinking coffee. I enjoyed being there by myself, having a little vacation from being mom and homemaker.

The area was full of tourists and conventioneers, but there were also quite a few homeless people who sat on benches or on the sidewalk. Some just hung out; a few tried to panhandle or just held cardboard signs.

If you intend to live in the Story that God is telling, and if you want the life he offers, then you are going to need more than a handful of principles, however noble they may be. There are too many twists and turns in the road ahead, too many ambushes waiting only God knows where, too much at stake. You cannot possibly prepare yourself for every situation. Narrow is the way, said Jesus. How shall we be sure to find it? We need God intimately, and we need him desperately.

—JOHN ELDREDGE[2]

One morning I sat and watched a thin woman in a dirty striped T-shirt flit from garbage can to garbage can, probing into each one like a bee gathering nectar from flowers. In one, she found a half-full cup of iced coffee. I watched her scoop the cup from the garbage, drain it in a single gulp, and politely toss the cup back into the garbage can. She scampered over to a friend—a young man with crutches who sat on the sidewalk with his homemade cardboard sign. She greeted him enthusiastically; they chatted for a moment. She moved on, looking for a little more breakfast.

I didn't know what to do. I wanted to listen to that moment, to hear what God had to say to me. It made me a little sad, watching the Christian conventioneers who avoided her gaze and gave her a wide berth as they walked down the street. It made me really sad that I sat drinking a $4 latte at Starbucks while she got her coffee out of the garbage can. I listened to the sense of injustice that rose up in me, to the desire to do something. But I felt frustrated and sad. I tried to just listen to that.

That day at lunch, meeting with another author, I had a salad I could not finish—one of those crazy oversized things with meat and cheese and vegetables in abundance. "Would you like me to wrap this up for you?" the waitress asked. I was on my way to yet another meeting and had no refrigerator. It would spoil if I took it with me. "I wish I could give it to a homeless person," I said. Well, it suddenly occurred to me: that wish, that desire, came from God. My saying, "I wish I could give it away," was God's way of saying, "Give it away." I listened to the sadness and love I felt that morning for that woman drinking coffee from the garbage, and to my own sense of helplessness. God responded by saying, "Give your lunch leftovers to a hungry person."

So I got the salad boxed up and was able to get a plastic fork and napkin from the restaurant. I walked down the street, eyeing street people.

I wasn't sure how to do this, so I asked God for help. The man I eventually gave my salad to seemed surprised, but he was a little out of it. He was sitting on the curb in an alley. He had long, stringy hair, baggy clothes. He was dirty, had scrapes and wounds, including one over his right eye. He looked a bit scary, especially to a suburban mom like me. But as I approached, the words "I was hungry and you gave me something to eat" kept going through my mind. I assumed this was the voice of love talking, so I went up to the man and said hello. When he looked up at me, he looked like Jesus. Not a pretty Jesus, not the flannel-graph Jesus of my youth. More like Jesus right after he's been beaten on his way to Calvary. "Are you hungry?" I asked the man; I repeated the question. He seemed confused, then nodded. "This is for you," I said, handing him the box. "God loves you."

There are so many homeless people in Denver. Giving a half-eaten salad to one of them doesn't make a dent in the social problem of poverty. At least, not a very big dent. I didn't solve that man's deepest need. But I listened to God, and that was a moment of connection, for me, with the voice of love—to risk, to do something outside my comfort zone. Some people thought I was crazy, told me I ought to have been afraid to talk to the man at all. But the voice that tells you to take a little bit of a risk and simply do something kind—I'm pretty sure that's God's voice.

So how do we tune in to that voice—the voice of love? I think we must learn to recognize both the voice of love and its opposite—the voice of fear.

Sometimes we get lonely or scared or feel like our life does not matter very much, that we're not important. Or life feels futile and pointless, at least at the moment. Or that homelessness and hunger are too huge to do anything about, so why even try? Or that poor people are dangerous and should be avoided. But the voice of love—that is, God's voice—says: "Just breathe, grace is sufficient, and you can hold on to that; you are the Beloved and you really do matter, and I've got something important for you to do." That something might be huge, or it might just be sharing your lunch or interacting with someone you ordinarily would avoid.

The rest of that week, I gave my leftovers to street kids. I did not preach; I just said, "God loves you and cares that you are hungry, so here." I wasn't trying to save the world; I was trying to listen and obey, to be just a tiny little light of grace and hope and kindness. It was one of the most deeply spiritual experiences I've had in a long while.

The voice of doubt and fear would tell me, don't bother. You can't make a difference, so why try? The voice of fear whispers that there is not enough—certainly not enough money or stuff, but on a deeper level it also claims that there is not enough love. And that the world is so dark and such a mess that any effort to let the light shine through is just futile. There just is not enough love or joy or purpose. Believing in scarcity will take us to a bleak place—a place where we start to think that if there is a bit of love and joy, there's not enough, so if someone else has those things, then there will be less for everyone, especially me. The universe's supply of love and joy and purpose will be depleted. There is simply not enough of anything.

The voice of love, on the other hand, says there is plenty. Come to the table where God is serving a feast. God is love and power and joy, and God is limitless. So the power and creativity and love and joy is limitless; and in fact, by listening to God's voice of love, we receive, and in so doing we create. We spread this love and power and joy by simply receiving it and realizing that there's enough to share.

What is your desire? What do you want to do that can simultaneously embrace what you love and move toward redeeming your struggles? God calls through our loves and our struggles for us to meet the world's needs. He has something for you to do—a holy calling. And your desire is what tells you the most about it. What is the desire of your heart?

∿ Acting on Your Desires ∿

The story of your life is shaped, not just by thinking about what you love, not just by talking about your pain. Both of these things shape our dreams, and then we have the opportunity to move forward—

to act, to do something to make the world a little more beautiful, to ask, What is my desire and what am I going to do about it?

Lawrice Flowers is someone who has decided to pursue his dreams, to do what he can to make the world a little more beautiful, in spite of the obstacles in front of him. According to the *Chicago Tribune,* Lawrice is growing up in a notoriously rough neighborhood on Chicago's south side. While his friends listened to rap music, he preferred classical. His grandmother had taught him to sing praises to God, had taken him to church. His love of music earned him a spot in the prestigious Chicago Children's Choir. It also earned him the disdain of some of his peers, who teased him, fought him, even threw rocks at him.

But he kept pursuing music and had recently been given an opportunity to go with the choir to Japan, to be one of the soloists at that concert. The problem was, his family could not afford to send him, even with scholarship help. According to the article, this hurdle didn't slow him down: "As he often did, Flowers asked God for help. That, after all, is how the music started. Growing up, Flowers danced his praises to the Lord with his grandmother, stomping his feet." The article went on to tell how this young boy kept working on developing his voice, and how his mother and grandmother hope that this opportunity will allow him to get out of the poor

 I believe that my deepest, truest desires are actually the Creator's desires for me. . . . your true desires are taking you along a continuum that leads to a wiser, truer you. Your deep desires are located in that well that is your very soul, and God created our souls to constantly move us toward health and wisdom and peace. Within your soul's mysteries is hidden the vision of what you are becoming.

—VINITA HAMPTON WRIGHT[3]

neighborhood when he grows up. He even found a creative way to finance his trip, with monthly payments, so that he could go to Japan. The article concludes: "When Flowers leaves for the week-long trip Tuesday, it will be the farthest from 56ᵗʰ and King that he has ever been. God, he says, was listening."[4]

Seems to me that Lawrice Flowers was listening to God, as well, when God told him, don't give up when people throw rocks at you or make fun of you for loving music. Don't give up just because you're $500 short for the trip of a lifetime. Let your deep desire shape the story of your life. Keep singing, keep believing, and I'll help you make the world a bit more beautiful.

A kid who lives in the projects, where he often hears gunfire outside his apartment, where he gets rocks thrown at him, might think the story of his life is pretty bleak. But not Lawrice Flowers. He's found God in his story, and he's telling that story with his life.

⌁ Finding Your Necessary Dream ⌁

At a recent conference, I heard speaker and consultant Nancy Ortberg speak about passion, gifts, and calling. "You have a necessary dream," she said. "Determining your calling is really hard work, but it is designed to make you alive to God."

She spoke about the "inexorable link between being and doing." Sometimes we have to simply be, but eventually, we have to do something with it, "to participate in God's work of redemption," she said.

What is your dream? In other words, what is your passion? What do you love to do? Ortberg also pointed out that many of us think that to really "serve" God we must move away from the things we love. But the fact is, we can serve within who God made us to be; we can live out the dream he's put in our hearts.

Your dream, what you love, has to do with the gifts God has given you.

The Bible gives these instructions for life: "Trust in the Lord and do good; dwell in the land and enjoy safe pasture. Delight yourself in the Lord and he will give you the desires of your heart" (Psalm 37:4).

In the doing good, in delighting yourself in God, in trusting that he won't call you to do something unless he also equips you to do it—that's where you'll discover the desires of your heart. God has put a dream in your heart, and when you delight yourself in him, focus on him, the dream, the passion, the desire for what he's put in you will become clear.

God already has plans for you. They may seem ordinary to you. Your dream may not have to do with full-time ministry or saving the world. But it may have everything to do with ministering to the people in your little corner of the world and saving just one or two other people—saving them from despair or loneliness or discouragement or an eternity apart from God. What things do you wish you could do to help others? That wishing is part of how God speaks to your heart, I think. Take time to notice the things God is doing in your life—the way he's growing you up, the circumstances he's using to shape your story. That will give you clues as to what God's purpose for you is. The Bible says, "For we are God's workmanship, created in Christ Jesus to do good works, which God prepared in advance for us to do" (Ephesians 2:10).

Do our tasks save us or earn us God's favor? No. The verse just before this one says that we've been saved by grace, not by our works. We've been given a great gift—an invitation to join God's family. Once in the family, we don't just sit there. We don't have to earn our way into God's grace, but once we've received it, what else would we do but respond by participating in the ongoing work that God is doing in the world? God has put dreams and desires in our hearts, and if we listen to our hearts, we will move toward doing the things that he has created for us to do. He's created them. The pressure's off. We just need to show up, sometimes in seemingly small ways, and pay attention.

> *Why are so many people bored or frustrated with their jobs? Why do they dread Monday morning and "thank God it's Friday"? Their hearts are not in their work. Far from it. However they arrived at what they're doing with their lives, it wasn't by listening to their heart. The same holds true for their love life. Why do so many relationships fail? Because one or both partners no longer have a heart for making it work. On and on it goes.*
>
> —JOHN ELDREDGE[5]

I am learning that listening to my life also includes listening to the deepest desire of my heart. What do you desire? What is your dream? Your passion? What do you want to do? What do you sense God is calling you to do?

We talked in the previous chapters about what you love and where you've struggled. Your desire takes both your loves and your struggles and redeems them by stepping out and doing whatever it is that God has called you to do. Your

desire embodies these things, puts them into action.

For example, I told you I love writing and books. Where have I struggled? I've struggled with believing in myself. For a long time, I thought the only legitimate jobs a writer could have were the ones most people think of as more "practical"—things like being a news reporter or a public relations specialist. For a few years, I actually wrote articles for magazines like *Roads and Bridges* and *Concrete News*—writing exciting stories about concrete paving projects and construction methods. I am not making this up.

Why? Because I knew I could write, and I figured I should do something "practical" that I'd get paid decently for. Only problem was, it was dehydrating my soul.

My desire is to write, to believe in myself enough not to give up when writing is hard and seems an illogical career choice. And to write things that seem to matter a little more than construction project updates.

But beyond just believing in myself, in my own writing, God has also used the story of my life to create a desire in me, a dream. I want to encourage other writers to embrace the creative life, to believe in themselves, to give encouragement, because I realize how precious that is. I want others to write, if that is what they believe God is calling them to do. And to write about things that they are passionate about, not what they think they "ought" to write. Julia Cameron, who writes about developing creativity, says this:

> One of our chief needs as creative beings is support. Unfortunately, this can be hard to come by. Ideally, we would be nurtured and encouraged first by our nuclear family and then by ever-widening circles of friends, teachers, well-wishers. As young artists, we need and want to be acknowledged for our attempts and efforts as well as for our achievements and triumphs. Unfortunately, many artists never receive this critical early encouragement. As a result, they may not know they are artists at all.[6]

For most of us, support comes in the wake of our success. But we need it sooner, when we are in the "attempt" stage. We may feel disappointed that we did not receive encouragement in the way we think we ought to have.

As a writer, I feel a deep desire to provide encouragement, as Cameron does in her book, to fledgling creative types who may not have received it elsewhere. Most artists (who may not even dare to call themselves that) encounter well-intended but misguided people who try to steer them toward more "practical" pursuits. They may even steer themselves that way, as I did. This has happened to all of us—people have valued our achievements more than our attempts, as Cameron points out. For all of our society's talk about "thinking outside the box," a lot of people get nervous if you actually do that.

So one of my passions, which gives me big clues about God's calling on my life, flows out of both my love and my struggle. It takes that love of writing and the pain of discouragement and my own fear, which I know other creative types struggle with as well. I want to write things that offer truth—which, even when it is difficult truth, will hopefully make the world a little more beautiful. I think that also, because I have longed for encouragement as a writer, I feel that part of my purpose is to encourage other writers.

God has been putting other writers in my path quite often lately. I don't think this is an accident but an affirmation of the dream he's put in me to let my work and my life encourage others, especially those who want to write but are afraid to do so. I know I must continue to write, not only to tell truth but also to lead others by example.

When I'm invited to speak on spiritual formation or to lead retreats on the spiritual life, there is inevitably someone in the audience who says, "Can I ask you about writing?"

And I listen. In this case, listening to other people is also listening to God. Often these fledgling writers ask, "How long does it take you to write a book?" I tell them that books simmer below the surface and it's hard to track the hours because sometimes ideas come in the middle of the night, and I'm also working the full-time job of running my household and caring for my family and am constantly interrupted. But I think, as I listen more deeply, that what they are looking for is an out. They want me to say it takes years, or eighty hours a week, or something (*anything!*) that will make it sound too hard. So they can sigh with relief and sadness and say, "I could never do that. It's impossible."

I refuse to tell them that. I say, "Write. You can write. Steal a few minutes each day and just do it. Keep writing."

Why do I say this? Because I am grateful that others have encouraged me. God gave me people, sometimes at just the right time, who affirmed that writing was one of my talents. A few people have spoken truth to me—loving, encouraging people who saw a gift and said, fan that into flame. Go ahead. Fear not, God is with you in it.

∿ Focusing on an Uncomfortable Word ∿

Depending on your upbringing, you may feel somewhat uncomfortable with the word *desire.* If you've focused on other people, you may not even know what you want or whether you are gifted to do anything.

I grew up in a rather conservative faith tradition, and no one talked about desire in the church I grew up in. Desire was equated with lust and dangerous emotionality. We were rational and logical Christian soldiers, disciplined and determined. I'm wondering if we really missed something.

I don't fault my church for taking this view. Many passages in the New Testament seem to be more focused on quashing desire, as in, don't give in to the desires of the flesh. And rightly so.

Look at Colossians 3:5: "Put to death, therefore, whatever belongs to your earthly nature: sexual immorality, impurity, lust, evil desires and greed, which is idolatry." If desire keeps company with a list like that, it must be all bad, right?

But there is within us a tension: the desires of our human, fallen self, and the desires of the Spirit, which wants what is good and right and life-giving. And if we have faith, God offers us the gift of the Spirit, in us, to transform our desires.

Romans 8:5 and 6 says: "Those who live according to the sinful nature have their minds set on what that nature desires; but those who live in accordance with the Spirit have their minds set on what the Spirit desires. The mind of the sinful man is death, but the mind controlled by the Spirit is life and peace."

It's tempting to oversimplify the whole thing, to imagine the Spirit and the Flesh, wresting for control, like those cartoons where Sylvester the Cat has an angel on one shoulder telling him, "don't eat Tweety bird," and a little devil on the other shoulder, telling him, "go ahead, that Tweety bird will be so tasty."

It's more than that, though. Listening to the voice of love— what the Spirit desires—is what will lead us to life and peace. And life is not just survival. It's not just keeping your nose clean. The Spirit is calling you to be a part of something bigger than yourself. You know it because it is in you, perhaps deeply buried but still there. You want to live life, *really* live it. You want what Jesus talked about—life to the full, life using your gifts to live out your dream, your passion. You want to make the world a little more beautiful.

How does God transform your desires? We may think our desires are for people to understand or respect us, for more power, or sex or money, a nicer house, or chocolate. Underneath those things there is a deeper, truer desire—a desire for freedom, significance, and purpose. Those are the desires that God puts in our heart and then promises to fulfill.

Perhaps in contrast to the New Testament, it seems to me that the Old Testament is much more comfortable with the language of desire. Just read Song of Solomon. But beyond that, it is full of promises that God will give us the desires of our hearts.

He forgives all my sins and heals all my diseases; he redeems my life from the pit and crowns me with love and compassion. He satisfies my desires with good things, so that my youth is renewed like the eagle's [Psalm 103:3–5].

Our desire redeems our life, renews our strength. And it helps others.

What is your desire? What do you really want? To figure that out, we have to look at where we have had three of our basic needs met: our need for freedom (to know that we are autonomous and truly have choices), our need for significance (when we have felt loved or important), and our need for purpose (that we are devoting our time and energy to something meaningful).

Part of listening to your life, listening to your desire, requires you to take a look at where you have found, or tried to find, these three things.

∿ Embracing Freedom ∿

Depending on your background, you may think of freedom as a good thing or a dangerous thing. If you grew up thinking God is all about the rules and keeping your nose clean, perhaps you didn't experience a lot of freedom.

Still, Jesus said, "You will know the truth and the truth will set you free." Free from what? It's more a question of free *to* what? Free to love other people, free to use your gifts to help and encourage and strengthen other people. And freedom begins with knowing the truth. In order to know it, we have to listen.

God speaks in many ways; we are free to listen or not. He does not coerce us to listen. He invites us. It is the only way to really give and receive love—in freedom.

I am free to listen, and to question, and to pay attention to my heart and the voice of my own gladness—the voice of my heart. It tells me about my giftedness but also, if I have just a little faith, it leads me to freedom.

If we have the truth in our hearts—that we are loved and we belong to Jesus—then we are free. But if we think that love is conditional, that we have to earn it, that it depends on us not messing up—where is the freedom in that?

I think many people feel trapped—by their jobs, family responsibilities, the maddening and ever-increasing pace of their lives. They have moments of escapism, like my fantasies of driving off into the sunset, but mostly, they feel stuck.

But what if you weren't stuck? What if you could see that you have choices? What if you could live your life embracing freedom instead of being weighed down by should's and ought to's?

> *I think Christian spirituality is like jazz music. . . . The first generation out of slavery invented jazz music. It is a music birthed out of freedom. And that is the closest thing I know to Christian spirituality. A music birthed out of freedom. Everybody sings their song the way they feel it, everybody closes their eyes and lifts up their hands.*
>
> —DONALD MILLER[7]

What changes would you make in your life if you could take one step back from other people's expectations of you and listen to the voice of your own gladness?

The voice of love is the voice of freedom. Maybe the last time you remember feeling free is running through the backyard barefoot in the summer when you were eight. Perhaps it was playing with your kids, or singing really loudly to music as you drove your car, or when you sat in the tub to unwind after a long day. Maybe it was when you threw yourself into a task, either at home or church or in the marketplace, and you felt like you were "in the zone." What is freedom, except shedding expectations and being who you really are?

As I write this, I am sitting in the backyard, listening to the warm spring wind in the willows. The chives in the planter boxes on my deck are topped with tightly loaded lavender buds, which will explode into furious purple puffballs in a day or two. The dog lounges in the corner of the deck as I write longhand, freed from the computer screen . . . for a while, anyway. And I do feel free— amazed that I get to do this, to write. A phone conversation this morning with a woman trying to listen to her life confirms that I'm going in the right direction with this book, and I'm thankful. I'm grateful for the task God's given me—to write encouragement to those who want to follow Christ.

Lately, I've also felt freedom in places where I have said no, as in, no, I can't do that for you; no, I am not going to be responsible for your feelings; no, I am not going to rescue you from the consequences of your own irresponsible behavior; no, I am not going to arrange my life around trying to maintain an image of perfection. I'm finding freedom, that is, in setting boundaries.

A mentor of mine once asked where I'd felt freedom. We then looked at the Bible, which says, "Where the spirit of the Lord is, there is freedom" (2 Corinthians 3:17). The converse, my mentor noted, was also true: where there is freedom, that's where the Spirit is. So if you are seeking God, trying to find where the Spirit might be, notice first where you felt most free. That's a good place to start looking.

∽ Seeking Significance ∽

There is a tension in desire; the desire for significance may take us along some strange paths. Many things—job, position, social connections, power, money—masquerade as the real deal when it comes to significance.

It's interesting to me what people will embrace in their search for significance. Often they will throw themselves into their career. They may pursue relationships, sometimes in an unhealthy way—trying to get into the right social circles, or just giving too much of themselves to the point of burnout. I've also seen people become work-a-holic volunteers, especially in ministry, as if this somehow earned them celestial brownie points or awarded them significance, like some carnival prize.

We often find it in relationship; as a parent or a sister or a friend, we give and receive love and affirmation. We are important in some way to someone else. There's nothing wrong with that. But we need more than just that.

The ultimate source for our significance is the fact that we are loved by God. Anything else just doesn't measure up. Because significance is based on *who* we are and *whose* we are, it cannot be based on what we do.

For example, Scot and I love to play tennis, so we joined a club near our home. I've made friends there and enjoyed the athletic activity. I have improved in my tennis abilities, and that feels good.

But I've noticed that there are people, especially women, who have turned tennis into their full-time occupation. They don't get paid for it; just the opposite. They spend staggering amounts of money on lessons, equipment, just the right outfit, in an attempt to get better at tennis. And when they win, they feel very significant. And when they don't, or if they don't make the right team, they are hurt.

I only know this because it is very easy for me to go down this same path, to listen to the voices that say, "Wow, you're really good at this; you are getting so much better. If you work really hard, someday you may get to be on the A team or play on Court One."

Good grief. What does that do for me? What unmet need am I trying to meet? Is success on the tennis court what I truly desire? Well, significance is what I truly desire—which, in itself, is not a bad thing. Still, if I believe that tennis, or my accomplishments at work, or the accomplishments of my children at school or in sports—if I think these things are a means to getting significance, then of course I will pursue them—sometimes to the detriment of my soul. While we may accomplish things that are significant, they may not be where we find our significance. That is found in the person we are becoming. Our experiences may shape us and help us in the process, but they are not the ultimate source of our significance.

If we focus solely on what we do, it won't ever satisfy us. There's a sort of hollowness, because you realize—okay, I've had this success in the workplace or my kid made the Little League all-star team—but it really doesn't give me what I had hoped it would.

How have you pursued significance? What have you learned along the way? When have you known most fully that you are significant? When have you known that you are loved? That you are important?

Asking those questions—without shame or blame, just observing the patterns—is part of how you listen to your life.

We all want to be wanted; we want someone to need us. But sometimes we find rather unhealthy ways to try to meet this need. It often puts us in relationships that can be damaging and, ultimately, make us feel not significant but simply used.

Maybe you pursue relationships with needy people. Or you think they just find you. You are the strong one, the pursuer, the initiator. You give, you listen. And then you get tired and simply withdraw. And then you feel guilty. You think your desire to be alone is wrong, that you ought to be—I don't know—nicer.

Don't get me wrong. We do need to listen to others. It's a good thing to be kind, but we also have to be kind to ourselves. One way to be kind to yourself is to listen to yourself, to your own life. And sometimes, we get so busy caring for others, way beyond a reasonable caring, that we can't hear what our own soul is whispering in our other ear—that this is not really working, it's not making me significant, it's just making me tired.

Allowing other people to use you, serving them so selflessly that you lose yourself—that doesn't make you significant. It makes you codependent.

We want to be valued. But we forget that God values us. He calls you beloved. And he has given you gifts and passions that will enable you to serve him with joy.

I find it hard to hear God, to pay attention to my passion, when the loud voices in my head, or my home, or my circles of friends seem to be saying something entirely different from what God is saying. So I wonder, To whom should I listen?

The tangible sound-wave voices hitting your eardrums seem more real than the still, small voice of God. You may even doubt that the quieter voice is real. But which voice calls you beloved and does so unconditionally?

If you are willing to give an ear to that small voice—the one that calls you beloved—if you can just give it a bit of attention, I think God rewards you with encouragement. The Spirit brings someone who echoes the truth—that you are called, and gifted, and significant. It takes you to the place where you can hear and heed the voice of your own gladness. The place where you are truly able to listen.

This may require you to say no to some people, to get some time alone, to take that time, which God is offering you, to just listen very quietly. It's hard to hear divine whispers amidst the noise or even in the just plain-old plain-oldness of it all. Find a quiet place where you can listen, where you can perhaps read a bit of scripture or just pour out your heart to God and then sit in silence and know he's with you. If it feels silly or unproductive to spend time in silence and quiet, do it just to humor yourself. Or to humor God—to offer the Spirit a landing strip in the uneven ground of your life. See what happens. God's is the only voice that will ultimately assure you of your significance.

∿ Finding Meaning and Purpose ∿

A lot of books about purpose and significance have hit the best-seller lists in recent years. *The Purpose-Driven Life, Your Best Life Now, The Search for Significance, From Success to Significance*—these are just a few of the titles that have been wildly popular. Why? I think we all are looking for meaning and purpose, and the oldest question in the universe is, Why am I here?

While significance is about who you are (you are loved, you are important), purpose is about what you are doing (I am loving, I am doing something important). Your purpose is your desire put into action. Significance and purpose are linked, just as being and doing are linked. Purpose is what we find when we do what God has given us the freedom to do, and we're able to because we know our significance. We find our purpose when we live out the desire that God has placed in our hearts.

It's about living beyond yourself. As Rick Warren points out in the opening chapter of his popular book,

> It's not about you. The purpose of your life is far greater than your own personal fulfillment, your peace of mind, or

even your happiness. It's far greater than your family, your career, or even your wildest dreams and ambitions. If you want to know why you were placed on this planet, you must begin with God. You were born by his purpose and for his purpose.[8]

Pretty amazing, isn't it? So what are we to do?

Don't rush. Take time to listen. As Warren points out, "The smile of God is the goal of your life."[9] And God smiles when we listen to the desires he's placed in us and move toward doing what will accomplish his purposes in the unique way he's gifted us to do.

The Bible says, "He has showed you, O man, what is good. And what does the Lord require of you? To act justly and to love mercy and to walk humbly with your God" (Micah 5:8).

What does the Lord require of you? What is your purpose? Certainly it's not just to think about what you love and to worry about your pain. It's a life in which we both be and do.

What would a life lived by the three statements in this verse from Micah look like?

• *To act justly.* That sounds good. We don't just say we like the idea of justice; we act justly. To act justly in a world where poverty and war and disease are rampant—if we really did that, our lives would look a bit different than they actually do, I think. This verse instructs us to do it. Act justly. Even in a small way, by sharing your lunch or a smile or being kind to someone it's not easy to be kind to. But don't just think about it. Act.

• *To love mercy.* What does it means to show mercy, not just think about it but to actually do it? Love mercy, but also be merciful. Mercy means not giving people what they deserve; it's letting them off the hook. How often do we do that when people wrong us? How often do we get distracted from the vision and purpose of our lives because we are mired in petty disagreements? This statement is really asking us to be like God, because God loves mercy. It's not something we can power up and make ourselves do. Our human nature doesn't naturally love mercy, except to love having it shown to us. The only way to do it is to let the Spirit control our desires. And that happens when we begin to live the final statement in this verse.

• *To walk with God.* The Bible is exhorting us to not simply think about God but to walk with him, to live our lives, moment to moment, in his presence; to invite God into the daily details of our lives; to do things with him, to let him direct us.

As we move forward, our purpose unfolds. God holds the plans and does not lay them all out before us. He tells us as much as we need to know and says, "Keep walking." Walk humbly with your God. Humble people don't demand all the answers but trust that God knows what's up and what to do. We don't walk alone; we walk with God—that means connecting and listening.

Often God will speak to us through other people. We'll hear a sermon, read a book, or just get a bit of good advice from a friend or even receive a nugget of truth from a child. Listening to other people is another way we can listen to God. It is to that practice that we will turn our attention in the next few chapters.

 Do you intend to live in the story that God is telling? What would that look like in your life? How might it be connected to making the world a little more beautiful?

What would it take for you to discover what your "deepest, truest desires" really are? Do you think your soul is moving toward "health and wisdom and peace"? Why or why not? What one step could you take toward discovering and naming your true desires?

What would it look like to listen to your heart? Would it take you to a place of freedom? Think about the story of your life—when was a time you listened to your heart? How might doing that help you find God in your story?

What comes to mind when you think about freedom? Do you agree or disagree with Miller's idea that Christian spirituality is "a music birthed out of freedom"?

PART II

LISTENING TO OTHERS

When we offer someone our undivided attention (and isn't that a gift that all of us long for?), we grow in the practice of love. Our careful listening to others has the power to transform us, to help us *become* more loving by simply *doing*. And if we practice loving, we become more Christ-like, because he is love. Our listening communicates love, often more clearly than our words. We are humbled; we realize, even as we practice, that we are not perfect listeners. We realize the things we say in response to others may carry not-so-hidden agendas. To truly listen, we must set aside our own junk—selfishness, neediness, overwhelming desire to interrupt with "that reminds me of what happened to *me!*"

Listening to others is fraught with complexity. While countless books have been written (and read) on the how's and why's of interpersonal communication, we still struggle with the basics: understanding others and getting them to understand us.

But even though it's difficult, it's worth doing, because when we listen, we often find God, in our own story and in the story of others. God speaks to us through other people. Listening to others intersects with listening to God, in at least two ways. First, our listening to others is a way God ministers *to them*—to have us be Christ to them. Most of us just want to be heard, to be understood. When we listen, we offer that gift of understanding to others. The goal of the Christian faith is to be like Jesus, to act as he would if he were in our place. And something I notice in Jesus' story is that he listened to people. So to minister to others, we can take a look at how he listened and do that for others. We can't just wish that into happening. But neither is it impossible. We simply have to practice it, and by practicing, we fine-tune our ability to hear others and God.

In order to be Christ to others we must listen, not only to the other person but also tune in simultaneously to God's whisper in our heart, giving us wisdom, giving us courage to set our own agenda aside in order to really love by listening. Taking the time to listen unhurriedly, to pray—these things will help us listen to others. Of course, being willing to do this often brings a deep satisfaction and joy. When we give, we receive.

Second, when we listen to others, they can offer us wisdom, a word from God, a question to ponder that will help us grow in some way. That is, God ministers *to us* through other people as they speak encouragement or exhortation. This ministry is not limited to words from a pastor or teacher, someone giving a lesson or a sermon. I think God often speaks to us through other people in casual conversation, through a child or someone unexpected.

Sometimes, this mutual ministry goes on simultaneously in a conversation—when I am willing to listen, to minister to someone by listening, I am sometimes surprised by God's kindness to me. I'm helped and strengthened by the conversation, by the other person's words but also by the fact that I was able to help someone by just giving them my attention.

There is a plethora of information out there on listening skills and techniques, and we'll review some of these to provide some context. I have found that for some people, these techniques feel awkward and difficult, so much so that they give up on using them. That is not to say that techniques don't have value, but unless you see the reason behind the techniques, they will forever feel awkward.

Learn all you can about listening skills; they are necessary. But our focus will be on the next step—applying those skills not to manipulate or just improve technique but to be transformed into a more Christ-like person, one who listens to God through others and shares God's love through the ministry of listening.

CHAPTER IV

Community: Listening Together

W hen we listen to the voice of love in our lives, what do we hear? We hear that we are loved, and then, that we ought to love others. One way to love is through the ministry of listening.

The Bible tells us that religious leaders in Jesus' day loved to debate—to argue over the finer points of the meaning of the Jewish scriptures, which they highly revered. Several times in the Gospels, we read about religious leaders asking Jesus, "Of all the commandments, which is the most important?" or, "Which is the greatest commandment?"

Look at how Jesus answers what they think is a trick question with great wisdom: "'Love the Lord your God with all your heart and with all your soul and with all your mind.' And the second is like it: 'Love your neighbor as yourself.' All the Law and the Prophets hang on these two commandments" (Matthew 22: 37–40).

The second command is "like" the first; in fact, it is the other side of the same coin. We can't love God and not love others—at least not authentically. When we love God, we also receive his love.

If we think we only love God and he does not love us in return, we're probably just offering God performance or legalism—not love.

God initiates love and listens to us first. That's what inspires us to love and to listen to God. The Bible says, "This is love: not that we loved God, but that he loved us and sent his Son as an atoning sacrifice for our sins" (1 John 4:10).

God listened to our dilemma and answered it with a loving sacrifice. And he asks us to share the love we've received with others; that's part of how we love God. The Bible goes on to say in the very next verse: "Dear friends, since God so loved us, we also ought to love one another. No one has ever seen God; but if we love each other, God lives in us and his love is made complete in us" (1 John 4: 11–12).

By loving others, we complete God's love. How do we give God's love to others? Listening is a very good place to start.

I so often think the words I give to people are more valuable than my quiet listening.

> *The first service that one owes to others in the fellowship consists in listening to them. Just as love to God begins with listening to His Word, so the beginning of love for the brethren is learning to listen to them. It is God's love for us that He not only gives us His Word but also lends us His ear. So it is His work that we do for our brother when we learn to listen to him. Christians, especially ministers, so often think they must always contribute something when they are in the company of others, that this is the one service they have to render. They forget that listening can be a greater service than speaking.*
>
> —DIETRICH BONHOEFFER[1]

But it is simply not true. Listening can be a greater service than speaking. And that is part of why we listen—because we are called to serve.

Jesus told his followers: "Whoever wants to become great among you must be your servant, and whoever wants to be first must be your slave—just as the Son of Man did not come to be served, but to serve, and to give his life as a ransom for many" (Matthew 20:26–27).

What does that mean, to serve? I don't think it's about indiscriminately allowing people to use us or about giving of ourselves endlessly. Serving is not about making everyone else happy. That's an impossible task. The great thing to me about serving by listening is that I don't have to come up with something profound. I don't have to solve the problem. I can just listen attentively, and that's enough. What a relief!

Of course, this is not always easy. Serving through listening is about being unselfish enough to not offer your advice. Giving your best self to others sometimes means letting go of needing to fix or advise them and just giving your attention, not giving with thinly veiled resentment, not giving when you have nothing in you to give. In order to give, we must first be filled. I find I am able to give my best self to others when I have taken care to listen first to God, to be filled with wisdom and strength beyond my own resources. Even Jesus took time to rest and relax. He also took time to actually stop listening to others for a little while so that he could listen to his Father—to get away so he could hear the voice of love clearly.

I think this is a great idea, but I don't always do it. I rush to help, to fix. I forget that I am a better listener, better equipped to help others, if I listen to God first.

I feel sometimes like the Samaritan woman at the well (see John 4:1–26). I think I'm doing Jesus a favor, offering him a drink of water, a listening ear. Turns out, his words are like living water. Hearing him, my soul is quenched.

With that full and satiated soul, I can then serve others. I can invite them to listen to Jesus, like the Samaritan woman did.

When I've spent some time listening to God, I'm better able to listen to his voice *as I listen to others.* This is truly what loving listening is about—listening to both God and the other person simultaneously. It's this combination, rather than my own efforts, that make listening a ministry.

Jesus was a loving listener. He was an active listener, not a passive one. Sometimes when he listened to people he argued with them or confronted them. He often taught by asking questions. But all the while, he listened closely to what people said, not just their words but the attitudes or feelings that were hidden behind those words.

Our listening, setting aside our agenda, is how we communicate to others their belovedness. This doesn't mean we always agree, or condone their behavior. We might lovingly confront them. But in that, we communicate God's love and attention.

We can only communicate that to others, however, if we know it is true of us—that we are the beloved of God. Letting others know that they are beloved as well—that is how we can be Christ to people who desperately need to make sense of their story by telling it to someone.

Henri Nouwen writes: "The greatest gift my friendship can give to you is the gift of your Belovedness. I can give that gift only insofar as I have claimed it for myself. Isn't that what friendship is all about: giving to each other the gift of our Belovedness?"[2]

After we have listened to God, to the voice of Love, we can listen to others from a place where our heart is full and satisfied. We can serve out of the abundance that God's love has created in us.

∾ Why Don't We Listen? ∾

If we know that listening is a loving thing to do and that it is helpful to others, why don't we do more of it?

Sometimes we are not sure how, or we think our advice is more helpful than our listening. Sometimes we are too quick to say, "I'll pray for you," and walk away. Sometimes the most helpful prayer is the one we say silently as we just sit with the person, giving our attention. Sometimes just listening to someone is a prayer. God speaks often through people, so listening to others share their pain or their insights is a form of listening prayer.

The Bible gives us good advice on how to listen: don't hurry to speak, even if you intend to give good advice or encouragement. Scripture warns us to be cautious about speaking, especially if you find yourself getting frustrated or angry: "My dear brothers and sisters, take note of this: Everyone should be quick to listen, slow to speak and slow to become angry" (James 1:19).

What does it mean to be quick to listen? James, who penned these words, knew from experience that life is hard. The opening chapter of his letter addresses life's tough issues: trials, doubt, poverty, temptation. He exhorts us to persevere in spite of these things. And then he reminds us to listen to each other. Why?

The less information we have about a given situation, the more likely we are to get angry, often about the wrong thing. If we can be slow to speak, if we wait to make sure we listen well and get all the information before talking, then we're less likely to get angry. Anger almost always leads to regret. We blow up, and then we're sorry, we regret it, we wish for longer fuses and better self-control. So take your time with speaking, which is easier to control than your anger. Slow down, breathe, and listen.

Have you ever had just enough information about a situation to get you mad? And you spout off or yell, only to find out more information that diffuses your anger. "Oh, that explains it," we say, embarrassed by our initial reaction. Wouldn't it be better to wait, to listen before we speak, because our anger can damage people? As James points out in the next verse, "anger does not bring about the righteous life that God desires" (James 1:20).

We are called to live by the Spirit, and the Bible says that a Spirit-led and empowered life will be increasingly loving, patient, kind, gentle, self-controlled (see Galatians 5:23). In other words, we will become more like Jesus. Listening to others, being slow to become angry, will allow the Spirit's fruit to flourish, for patience and love and kindness to grow in us.

Where else in the Bible do we see that phrase, "slow to anger"? It is contained in one of my favorite descriptions of God, appearing numerous times throughout scripture. "The Lord is compassionate and gracious, slow to anger, abounding in love" (Psalm 103:8 and elsewhere).

"Slow to anger" is one of three parallel statements about God. The other two phrases, "abounding in love" and "gracious and compassionate," are facets of his character. To be loving and compassionate means you will be slow to anger. These qualities are inextricably wound in the nature of God and in the nature that the Spirit is creating in us.

The point of allowing the Spirit to pervade our lives, to live through us, is so that we will be transformed. And transformed into what? Into someone who is more like the God we follow and worship. More compassionate and gracious, abounding in love, slow to anger. Does that describe me? On a really good day (or good moment), maybe. Not always, not consistently. But listening is a spiritual practice that can move me in that direction.

The Christian faith is a journey, a process. We're never done, at least not in this life. We are moving toward being more like Jesus. Even when it seems like we are not moving forward, I think we're still on the journey. We're just learning things the hard way.

While we are being conformed, that is, changed, into the *image* of Christ, we never arrive at some mysterious station where we *become* God. God is the intimate other—in my thoughts and heart, even in my actions, yet distinct and independent of me. God is Creator; I am a created being. I reflect him. As I listen, I need to hold that paradox before me: I'm not God, but I can act in a Christ-like manner in any number of ways, including by listening to others' pain or to their joys and rejoicing with them.

The Bible says we ought to "Rejoice with those who rejoice; mourn with those who mourn. Live in harmony with one another" (Romans 12:15–16). I think to do that, I need to really listen to people. I can't always get it right; I'm not God, but I can and should ask myself how I can come alongside someone who's in pain, in a loving way, in a how-Jesus-would-do-it sort of way. How can I love as Jesus would love? How can I love this person as if she were Jesus?

Another reason we don't always listen is because we have learned not to do so. It is an exhausting daily battle for many of us just to figure out which of the many voices around us we ought to listen to. We are overwhelmed with information and noise, and we are moving quickly through the jungle of information and misinformation. To survive, we have learned to selectively ignore.

Let me illustrate. When you are driving, you are likely to have any number of distractions, from billboards to the radio to the other drivers to the cell phone to the screaming kids in the backseat of your car. In order to drive safely, you have to be selective about which of the many things you see and hear that you will pay attention to. If you give your full attention to billboards, you

> *Spiritual formation is the process of being conformed to the image of Christ for the sake of others.*
>
> —ROBERT M. MULHOLLAND JR.[3]

won't be watching the road and the cars around you. If you turn around to give all of your attention to your children in the backseat, the results could be disastrous. Because of the accidents caused by drivers distracted by cell phones, using them while driving is against the law in a growing number of cities, including Chicago.

> *"Be quick to listen" is not something to which we are to passively assent or to smile and say, "It sure would be nice if everybody listened like that." It's an active and unconditional command. Obedient Christians who read these words can't be passive about how they connect with God or other people. For in addition to "loving the Lord our God," Jesus goes on to command us to love our neighbors as we want to be loved ourselves (Mark 12:31). In order to satisfy our own deep longing to be heard, then, we need to equip ourselves to truly listen to others.*
>
> —DAVE PING AND
> ANNE CLIPPARD[4]

If you need to find a certain street to turn on, you need to give your attention to the signs that direct you. You may at times give attention to the people in the car with you, but sometimes you have to stop listening to them, even asking them to stop talking so you can concentrate on the traffic or finding your way. You have to ignore certain things sometimes to survive.

In our lives, there's so much noise we can't pay attention to all of it. This means developing discernment about when to listen and when to ignore.

But we sometimes get too good at ignoring, and we miss the chance to really listen to others, to show them love. Listening to others requires effort. It is hard work to really pay attention. But it is the most important thing we can do for each other, and it is a way to develop our ear so that we can better hear God.

Doing the hard work of listening to others—loving others by offering them our attention—will help us become better listeners. And if we are better listeners, we will be better able to listen to God. And I don't know about you, but that's what I want: to hear God more clearly.

∿ What Is Active Listening? ∿

Loving listening is active listening. When I lead retreats, I sometimes have participants do an exercise to help them improve their listening skills and also to show them how listening and love are related. One person in the group shares a part of her story, usually a decision she is facing.

The rest of the group must listen. They may ask questions to clarify, but mostly they are to listen actively, to reflect back what the person is saying, to communicate caring, warmth, and empathy with their body language and facial expressions. They are told not to give any advice or try to direct the person in any way but simply to listen, with an ear to God, to encourage and help that person seek clearness on the issue she is facing.

If the participants in the group are able to keep themselves from judging or advising (which, by the way, most find excruciatingly difficult), they often are surprised by how the exercise affects them. The one who is listened to often realizes that she has rarely (sometimes never) been listened to in quite this way before. "I felt like they really heard me," I often hear. Some are so used to getting advice that they are a bit uncomfortable in not being told what to do. Others don't like the fact that people are asking them questions, gently taking them to a place where they have to examine their motives and deep feelings. It can be a bit scary to have to look at ourselves honestly.

But if she can push through that, the person who is listened to will often find that she feels loved as a result of being heard without judgment. Those who listen find it difficult sometimes to break old patterns of interrupting and advice-giving but realize that the gift of listening is not in the fixing of people but in the walking beside them, in the empathy.

For many of us, active listening is difficult. Active listening means we are not just waiting for the other person to stop talking. We are paying attention. We give the person feedback, in the form of paraphrasing what's been said, or by nodding, or making eye contact. We face the person and, by our expression and body language, communicate warmth, caring, and attention.

Many people I talk to, especially married couples, have a hard time with listening to each other in this way. When instructed to "mirror" or "reflect" back what someone is saying, they say, people will say it sounds strange and repetitive. When we have to listen and then give feedback by saying things like, "I hear you saying that . . ." or "it sounds like you are feeling . . ." we balk, saying it is too awkward to listen in this way.

But almost any new skill feels awkward at first. Listening is hard work. But it is a means to an end. Listening is a way to love. Love is not just a warm, fuzzy feeling we can conjure up in our minds or hearts. Love is sacrifice. And listening, especially in a way that requires us to be engaged, to participate—that's not always easy.

But real love calls us to listen, even if it requires effort on our part.

"Real listening requires a level of sacrifice," write Ping and Clippard. "It means dying to ourselves and our agendas. Listening also teaches us humility by confronting us with the embarrassing reality of how little we actually know and how little power we truly have to change other people's lives."[5]

Did you catch that? *How little we actually know.* Why is that hard to admit? Our culture values information and reveres "experts." Still, while many of us would rather not admit how little we actually know, there is a certain freedom in it. We don't have to have the answers; we simply trust that God has them and will reveal them at the proper time. We can never love perfectly, but God can love others through us when we listen to them.

And he can love us through others in that exchange as well. When we listen deeply, we are able to invite God into the exchange. The paradox of giving away our life to find it is deeply embedded in the act of loving listening.

We often say we want to follow Jesus' example by serving others. I believe that one of the best ways we can do that is to offer to listen to them. When someone talks to you, look the person in the eye and say, "Really. Tell me more about that." And then really listen. You will be surprised at how this affects people and how much they will tell you.

Take a genuine interest in people. If that's difficult for you, *act* as if you are interested. Your feelings will follow your action. Just ask yourself, if I really did care, if I were really interested, what would I do? Amazingly, your heart will begin to soften when you "act as if" you are a good listener. God is counting on you to love others for him, and listening to them is the first step toward that.

∿ How Do We Actually Do This? ∿

So, how does this play out in our listening to others, in our real-life interactions, in our relationships? How do we listen with this kind of compassion? To start with, before we ever have a conversation with anyone, we need to have a conversation with God.

Pray, even if just for a few moments before talking with someone. Wait for God's prompting before you speak. Don't be afraid to be quiet for a moment, to create some space for the person to talk and for God to act. This will feel uncomfortable, perhaps, but if you allow yourself to be comfortable with silence, the other person may feel that as well.

Listen empathetically. Get out of your own head. Focus on what the other person is saying, not only with his words but with his body language, tone of voice, even the look in his eyes. Have you ever had someone tell you, "I'm fine, really," but his eyes had such pain and anxiety that you knew he was not fine at all? Be willing to just ask, "Really? Are you doing okay? Do you need to talk?" And then be willing to listen patiently.

I had breakfast with a friend the other day, and as we talked, I kept hearing myself say, "I know what you mean. Like when I . . ." and then I would stop. I was frustrated by how often I started talking about myself. But I kept reminding myself, this friend often listens to you. Give her the gift of listening to her. Ask questions, and just listen. Give her the gift of your attention.

Each time I gently reminded myself to not talk about myself, it got easier. Eventually, I got caught up in her story and her struggle and didn't even think about my own stuff. At the end of breakfast, she said, "We didn't even talk about what's going on with you." I just smiled. "Next time," I said. We know there is give and take in our relationship.

When you listen, don't just avoid talking about yourself. Don't just smile and nod. Pay attention. Communicate care and warmth with your body, your expression. I remember a small-group leader I worked with who was a terrific leader because she would really listen. She'd even make these encouraging little sounds as she listened: "Mmmm," she'd say, nodding and making eye contact. "Uh-huh," she'd encourage someone, when there was a pause. You just wanted to talk to her.

Depending on which case study you look at, experts say that more than half of what we communicate to others comes, not through our words but from body language and another sizable chunk from our tone of voice. Our actual words really only make up a very small part of the message.

If this is true, we need to learn to listen to nonverbal and tone clues. If someone says, "Yeah, right!" she could mean she totally agrees with you or she completely disagrees with you, depending on her tone and her expression. So being quick to listen means paying attention to what a person's tone, demeanor, and body language are saying; they are usually more reliable sources of information than words.

Don't use the time that the other person is talking to carefully craft your brilliant answer to solve the problem being described. Use it to listen fully. Engage. Do those little noises like that small-group leader, if you can. Occasionally paraphrase: "It sounds like you are feeling . . ." or "I hear you saying . . . is that right?"

As I said earlier, this is sometimes awkward. But it is loving. To listen empathetically is to love someone the way you would like to be loved. It requires us to slow down. It's hard to listen deeply in a hurry. It is what Jesus asked us to do when he said, "Love your neighbor as yourself."

Use eye contact and your own body language to convey warmth, caring. For example, face the person. Think about it. Which feels more welcoming: someone turned slightly away with arms and legs crossed or someone who is sitting with an "open" posture, perhaps leaning forward slightly, looking you in the eye?

∽ What If This Were Jesus? ∽

For some people, asking themselves, What would Jesus do? is helpful in knowing how to treat people in any interaction, especially in listening. I find that I sometimes feel overwhelmed trying to do what Jesus would do. It's a pretty high standard, and it can seem unattainable on days when I'm feeling a bit cranky.

When that happens, I change the question to something that might not have as catchy an acronym but for me is more accessible. I ask, What if this were Jesus? Because I have a relationship with Jesus and I want to love him (usually more than I want to love difficult people), I find that this question helps me to be a bit more patient. What if this crabby child were Jesus? What if this impatient person at work were Jesus? How would I treat these people? How would I listen?

Now, sometimes this is a stretch. I don't think Jesus would tell me the type of things my kids sometimes talk to me about. He'd be deeper, and he'd use better grammar. But what happens to my relationship with my child if I try to listen to her the way I would listen to Jesus, even when she wants to tell me a very long and convoluted story (usually while I am driving or trying to cook dinner) that may sound like: ". . . And so she goes, 'well, I can't believe it' and I'm like, 'right,' and then she told me that Claire was not going to hang out with us on the playground because she wants to hang with someone else and I'm like, 'with WHO?' And she goes, 'well, who do you think?' And I'm like, 'ohmigosh' and she's like, 'right, totally!' Can you believe that, Mom? She just thinks she's all that, you know?"

Okay, maybe it's not that bad. Or maybe it's worse—your kid wants to give you a blow-by-blow summary of today's *Dora the Explorer* plot. Or someone with a lot of aches and pains wants to tell you about all of them. Or a coworker wants to complain about her latest project or tell you why it's unfair she got passed over for a promotion. What if Jesus wanted to talk to you about these things? Could you listen?

The Bible says that when you do things for others, it's as if you are doing them for Jesus. So when you listen kindly to others, you are listening to Jesus. It's in that act that he will meet you and speak to you, if not with words then with the joy of knowing that you have shared his love with someone.

Ironically, when we listen to people as if they were Jesus, we end up listening like Jesus would. We are more patient and kind than we would be just by trying to be nice.

Listening communicates love. Through it, we provide love to someone. Sometimes that means just receiving, sometimes it means confronting them with truth, sometimes it means saying, "I understand." God may unexpectedly give us someone who brings encouragement or strength, and we receive love through their words. In any (and every) conversation, we can

In spiritual listening . . . it is to God that we want to direct our listening ears. As you listen, the goal is to help the other listen to the Spirit of God who dwells within. The listener is a vessel of his grace. The conversation in which we are engaged is an on-going one between God and the other person. It does not begin with us. It does not end with us. In spiritual listening, Jesus himself is the Alpha and the Omega, the beginning and the end.

—ALICE FRYLING[6]

know that we are a part of the connection between God and his people—a connection of love that begins with listening to each other.

Has anyone ever shown you love by simply listening to you? What was that like? How did you feel about it? Have you ever tried to serve someone simply by listening?

How might listening to others play a role in your spiritual formation? How might their listening to you help you to be conformed to the image of Christ?

What does it mean to be "quick to listen"? Do you think of it as one of God's commands? How, specifically, could you equip yourself to truly listen to others?

When you listen to someone, what would you have to do, or not do, in order to be a vessel of God's grace? What does it really mean to invite Jesus into the midst of a conversation?

CHAPTER V

Compassion:
Suffering Together

A few years ago, my husband's youngest brother died suddenly of a massive heart attack. He was only thirty-four.

His family was bewildered and sad, losing the youngest of five siblings. The pain was so great, they had to hold it at arm's length. Shock doesn't even begin to describe it.

Tom's death was hard on us as a couple as well. My poor husband felt a million things, from guilt that he hadn't been closer to Tom, to frustration and anger that there was nothing he could have done to protect his little brother from such a tragic end.

I didn't know quite how to respond. Most of us don't handle tragedy with the grace we think we ought to. Perhaps you are at your best in the face of unspeakable, senseless, tragic loss, but I am not. In the first few weeks after Tom's death, I was frustrated to notice that Scot and I were arguing more than normal, that he seemed to me impatient and ungrateful for my attempts to comfort him. I got mad at him for small things he did. I think I was not handling my grief very well either.

I was talking to a friend about the situation, about how helpless I felt and how angry Scot seemed, how we were bickering for no reason. I felt like everything I said just made him angry. I felt bad, but I was getting tired of his anger. I was getting a little testy myself.

"I wonder," my friend said, "what it would look like to extend grace to your husband while he's grieving?" Extend grace? Forgive the fact that in the face of unimaginable tragedy he was not his normal cheerful self? Hmm. I was a bit embarrassed that I hadn't thought to give such a basic gift myself.

The Bible tells us, "Therefore, as God's chosen people, holy and dearly loved, clothe yourselves with compassion, kindness, humility, gentleness and patience. Bear with each other and forgive whatever grievances you may have against one another. Forgive as the Lord forgave you" (Colossians 3:13).

I decided to listen to the voice of God, which came through the gentle question of my friend. I knew I needed to simply listen to Scot. To be gracious and compassionate, slow to anger, rich in love. Whether I felt like it or not, I needed to forgive him, not because I was so noble but because I was so forgiven myself. To say, "Of course you are angry. Death just kicked you in the gut and walked away laughing."

I prayed that I would not pick up the gauntlet when it felt like Scot was throwing it down, that I would be kind (even if being kind meant just saying nothing) instead of engaging in a fight. I asked heaven for help in being just a little bit gracious. Now, I didn't do it perfectly. But I really tried. Which means, I walked away and bit my tongue a lot. The amazing thing was, God took my little ember of patience and grace and blew gently on it so that it warmed and, eventually, got a little flame of love going in my heart. My change in attitude didn't take away Scot's pain. Really, it helped me more than him. To let go of my need to be right actually made me a safer person for Scot. He was able to process some of the grief with me and even more of it with other people who came alongside him.

You'd think I would automatically extend grace to my husband. I mean, if an acquaintance, rather than my spouse, had suddenly lost a sibling, wouldn't I be patient and gentle with that person? Wouldn't I try to at least act like a Christian? Why was it so difficult to be deliberately kind to the man I love?

Unfortunately, we're often hardest on the people who are closest to us. We hear more of their words, but we don't always listen to what's really going on. As I tried to listen to Scot, to understand that his anger really wasn't directed at me, things improved. When he realized that I wouldn't pick on him during that time, it freed him up to work through the sadness—to be able to put his emotional effort into grieving instead of arguing with me.

It was not easy, extending grace. But it was healing, not only for Scot but for me. I realized that this was how I ought to be living my life all the time, not just in a season of pain. Because life has painful moments on a regular basis, and, God knows, we need all the grace we can give to each other.

Listening to others in pain sometimes means listening to how crabby they are, how they really *don't* want to talk about it, and being okay with that, at least for now. Listening means hearing what they say and realizing they don't intend to hurt you, that they are just wounded and need some time to heal.

Sometimes, we are called upon to listen to a confession. James 5:16 says, "Therefore confess your sins to each other and pray for each other so that you may be healed."

When someone comes to us to share a confession, we should treat the person with respect and grace. We can't just say, "Oh, that sin doesn't matter." Because it does. One of my closest friends, when I apologize to her for something I've done to hurt her or confess some other mistake, will often offer this wise and kind response: "Keri, what I love about you is that your sin really bothers you."

She's certainly not sweeping my mistakes under the rug, but she's not condemning me either. Her words sometimes sting a little—but in a good way, like antiseptic. She's cleaning out the wound, affirming that I need to turn things around, make amends, whatever. And then she forgives—and it means something because she didn't say, "Oh, it was nothing." It wasn't nothing. It was something, and that makes forgiveness that much sweeter.

This type of listening to confession and extending forgiveness is how we obey the Bible's direction to "Be kind and compassionate to one another, forgiving each other, just as in Christ God forgave you" (Ephesians 4:32).

Compassion is a gift we give others and that comes back to us. We learn that we are not made to fix others, because that is God's job, and God is actually very good at that. We learn that we are not alone, that pain can be what connects, rather than isolates, us. Compassionate listening also gives us an opportunity to extend grace to others and thus grow in grace ourselves.

As we grow toward Christ, we will build community with those we listen to. Within that community, we listen to God together and call forth the best in each other.

∿ Come-Alongside-ness ∿

When I was growing up, I heard a lot of talk at church about "the great commission"—to go and make disciples (Matthew 28:19). Different people interpret what that means in different ways. Some seem to think it means just getting people to convert to Christianity, to start a relationship with Christ. My own church growing up put quite an emphasis on the conversion experience, which usually had to be preceded by convincing someone to believe in Jesus. This is not a bad thing, but I think there needs to be more to it than just that. If you read all of Jesus' last words in

Matthew, it says he wanted his followers to make disciples, baptize them, and "teach them to obey everything I have commanded you." And what was his greatest command? Love God and love others. That's not just starting a relationship. That's keeping it going.

To teach people to love, you can't just tell them they ought to love. You have to love them, to teach by example. So to me, the most effective way to make disciples is not to argue with them or merely convince them that you are right but to listen to them. It means coming alongside people, hearing their story, and finding God at work in their story, and pointing it out to them—to say, "It sounds like you are on quite a journey and that God has been with you in that." Because God is at work in the hearts of people, even before they are aware of it. Even if the person you are speaking to hasn't identified that presence as God, the beginning of discipleship is to help that person notice the activity of God in everyday experience.

A few days before he died, Jesus told his followers, "Because I have said these things, you are filled with grief. But I tell you the truth: It is for your good that I am going away. Unless I go away, the Counselor will not come to you; but if I go, I will send him to you" (John 15:6–7). The word we translate as "Counselor" is, in the Greek, *Paraclete*. It means someone who comes alongside. (We get words like *parallel* and *paraphrase* from the same root.) *Paraclete*—God who comes alongside us. Which is what a good counselor does—comes alongside us and walks with us, listens, and guides. Jesus was talking about the Spirit, which comes alongside us and lives in us, listening and guiding us.

Just as the Spirit comes alongside us, we can love others by coming alongside them. How? By being compassionate. The word *compassion* comes from two Latin words, *cum* and *pati,* which point to the word's meaning, "to suffer with."

If we are led by the Spirit, we will increasingly imitate God and become people who are filled with "come-alongside-ness." That is, we listen to God and people and then come into their story, get involved with them enough that we can point out where God is in their story and allow them to do that for us as well. When we are full of come-alongside-ness, we will be willing to walk with people through their pain; we will listen before we try to fix. We will be with people. We might come alongside them in a church or a small group, where we try to learn and pray and encourage each other to grow in our faith. We might come alongside friends who are still trying to find God or who don't think they even have any interest in God and become a loving part of their story.

Now, I am not always as compassionate as I'd like to be. But listening is a spiritual practice that helps my compassion grow. When I am quick to listen and slow to anger, I can let God in to change my desires to match the Spirit's desires. I can be transformed (slowly, I admit!) into being more like Jesus. The Bible says that "those who live in accordance with the Spirit have their minds set on what the Spirit desires" (Romans 8:5). The Bible also reminds us that if we have been adopted into God's family through Jesus, we are changed; we have a new nature: "You, however, are controlled not by the sinful nature but by the Spirit, if the spirit of God lives in you" (Romans 8:9). This doesn't mean we never make mistakes, but we are in the process of becoming more like the Spirit that lives within our hearts.

Other people are in that process, too. Sometimes "coming alongside" means listening as someone confesses weakness or mistakes or just hearing the person's point of view. It usually requires that we pay attention, not just to the situation being described at that moment but to the person's whole story. Knowing where God has been in that story up to now will often give us clues about the best way to be compassionate.

∿ Brokenness ∿

When people know your story, they can listen to it and speak into it in a way that may help heal some of the brokenness that is an inevitable and inextricable part of life. They can help you find God in your story. That's how listening and compassion intertwine.

My friend Lindy Lowry is a magazine editor. We met when I was writing an article for her. We got to know each other a bit, shared our stories. Lindy says the listening ministry of a community of friends may have saved her life. Their ability to listen told them how to be compassionate, how to come alongside Lindy at a time she desperately needed it.

While she was in college, she was a part of a community of Christians—a group of friends who loved and encouraged and listened to each other. These friends knew Lindy's story—how she'd met Jesus when she was a ten-year-old at a Christian camp, through the stories from C. S. Lewis's *Chronicles of Narnia*, how she loved to think and read and write, how she loved Jesus.

But the summer she was twenty, Lindy's story took an unexpected turn for the worse. She had stayed at college to take summer school classes. Back in her small Texas hometown, her best friend was kidnapped, raped, and brutally murdered. The horrible crime rocked Lindy's faith.

"It was a crisis of faith unlike anything I've ever experienced," she says. Her friends watched sadly as Lindy rejected her faith, began to live as if God did not exist, as if her actions had no consequences. She rebelled, both in lifestyle and in her heart and mind. She was just plain angry at God, couldn't understand why God would allow her friend, a Christian, to be the victim of a senseless and brutal crime—killed by being stabbed ten times.

"The God I had believed in as a child seemed to be about making everything okay," she said. "He was supposed to be a friend. Well, this is not something a friend would do. It flew in the face of all that I had heard about God."

For about a year and a half, Lindy remained angry; she kept living a rebellious lifestyle. But her Christian friends did not give up on her. They listened to her pain, her questions. They stayed with her.

One friend in particular listened very deeply, not just to the present situation but to Lindy's life. She knew Lindy well enough, having listened to her story and remembering what had first brought Lindy to Christ: the stories in C. S. Lewis's *The Chronicles of Narnia*. She'd met Christ through the fictional character of Aslan the Lion, the Christ-figure in Lewis's stories.

So her friend got the books and started reading them. In the seventh and last book in the series, Lewis uses the story to give a wonderful picture of heaven. She gave the book to Lindy to read, reassuring her that her friend was now in heaven. She invited her to a Bible study on the topic of heaven that she and a few others in their community had put together with Lindy in mind. She also showed her the passage in the first book where the main characters—four children—are first told about Aslan (in a conversation with talking Beavers). When they realize that Aslan is a Lion, they are apprehensive. Here's the passage Lindy's friend showed her:

> "Ooh!" said Susan, "I'd thought he was a man. Is he—quite safe? I shall feel rather nervous about meeting a lion."
>
> "That you will, dearie, and no mistake," said Mrs. Beaver. "If there's anyone who can appear before Aslan without their knees knocking, they're either braver than most or else just silly."
>
> "Then he isn't safe?" said Lucy.
>
> "Safe?" said Mr. Beaver. "Don't you hear what Mrs. Beaver tells you? Who said anything about safe? 'Course he isn't safe. But he's good. He's the King, I tell you."[1]

"My friend said to me, 'I don't pretend to know what you're going through, but I thought this would be helpful,'" Lindy says. "It resonated with me. God was no longer safe. But I realized that maybe that's not what God is all about. It didn't fix everything, but it was a turning point. It started me on a path, exploring who God is. I began to embrace the beauty and the mystery of God, realizing I couldn't know everything about him or why he did what he did."

Lindy went to the Bible study about heaven, reading the Bible again for the first time in a long time. Through the study, she was able to both listen and be listened to. Her friends continued to be there for her as she tried to forge a more mature faith in a God who was not safe, but good.

"They were good friends who came alongside me," Lindy says. "But they waited. If she had come to me immediately, I

God has put this Word into the mouth of men in order that it may be communicated to other men. When one person is struck by the Word, he speaks it to others . . . . Therefore, the Christian needs another Christian who speaks God's word to him. . . . And that also clarifies the goal of all Christian community: they meet one another as bringers of the message of salvation.

—DIETRICH BONHOEFFER[2]

might not have listened. She also was wise. She chose a tool that I would identify with. She knew I loved books, that I loved those books especially. She knew I'd read the books before I'd be willing to read the Bible again. She knew me; she knew my story and paid attention to it, and that helped."

Lindy's friends helped her reconcile to God. They brought the message of salvation back to her, in a way that fit into her story, that made sense to her. They helped her, slowly, to be reconciled to God. But sometimes, listening is a way that we can be reconciled to each other.

∽ The Ministry of Reconciliation ∽

I have a photo on my desk of my brother and my two children, sitting on the front steps of our house. It's dear to me, and I want to tell you why. It's a photo that never would have been taken if I hadn't listened.

When my second child was almost a year old, I realized my brother had never even met him. I was frustrated because my brother, being single and living far away, didn't understand why he ought to see my kids. In one difficult conversation, he pointed out that I hadn't been out to see his new house, so why should he come see my new baby? I thought a baby was a little more important than a house, but he didn't see it that way.

So I didn't have that great of a relationship with my brother. I wished we could be closer, that we could be less competitive, that we could be better friends, at least. We had never had a big falling out (although I was sort of mad the year he sent me a Chia pet for Christmas). We'd just drifted, had a few minor misunderstandings. So now, I just wished we could be closer, that we could have a relationship in which he would care that I'd had a baby and want to see my child.

I prayed about it and asked God to fix my brother, if the truth be told. Well, God sort of laughed and led me to a passage in the Bible: "If anyone is in Christ, he is a new creation; the old has gone, the new has come! All this is from God, who reconciled us to himself through Christ and gave us the ministry of reconciliation: that God was reconciling the world to himself in Christ, not counting men's sins against them. And he has committed to us the message of reconciliation" (2 Corinthians 5:17).

Well, I listened to God through that verse. That word, *reconciliation,* filled me with a longing. I wanted to be reconciled to my little brother. We'd had a typical sibling relationship growing up—sometimes close, sometimes fighting, often jealous but also caring. In our family, I had been the overachieving perfectionist oldest child, and he had been the rebellious trouble-maker—or at least that's how people saw us. This is a formula for resentment on both sides. Still, we'd managed to be pretty close through high school and college.

But lately, it seemed like there was a lot of tension and distance, if those things can coexist. I had thought about continuing to ignore it. After all, he lived on the other side of the country. He's my only sibling, though, so I wanted a better relationship. I tried to listen to that desire. I wanted him to come and see me and my children, but he wasn't going to. But through the verses in Corinthians and the angst in my heart, God seemed to be saying, Hey, I've made you a new person, I'm not counting your sins against you, and I've given you a ministry of reconciliation. If I can do that for you, you should do it for your brother.

This process didn't happen quickly. It took a few months. I have to give my husband, Scot, a lot of credit. When I told him I needed to fly to Phoenix (in August, no less) to try to take a step toward healing my relationship with my brother, leaving him to care for the kids who were one and three years old at the time, he said okay.

When my parents heard of my plans, they called, worried. "Why are you going to see Kirk? Is everything okay?"

So I went to Phoenix, and within the first hour, my brother said, "So, why are you here?" I replied, "I want to have a better relationship with you, because the one we have right now is pretty pathetic. I want to be closer to you."

He looked surprised, but then he smiled. "Okay," he said.

That weekend, we reconnected. I came alongside my brother, lived in his world, saw his new house, admired his decorating, affirmed his success. I went to his office with him and watched him work the phones, selling stocks. I was amazed, really, at how good he was at his job. I did a lot of listening, not just to him but to his life.

I really tried to see things from his perspective. I asked questions and attempted to listen without judgment. We talked about our growing up and those awkward years after college, as both of us tried to find our place in the world (he'd had a few false starts in the career department before he discovered stock brokering). I got some of the missing pieces of information that really helped me to understand him and his choices a lot better. When he realized I wasn't going to judge him, he offered a glimpse of some of his pain. I realized we had more in common than I had thought.

I also got to meet the woman he eventually married, since he was dating her at that time. My brother took us boating on a reservoir outside Scottsdale, and she and I sat on the boat and chatted. I liked her. The only advice I gave him the whole weekend was about her: "Don't let this one get away, Kirk. There aren't many women who could put up with you."

Not long after my trip, my brother came to Chicago to see some of his old friends, including me. We took the picture of him with the kids on the front steps—a picture of reconciliation.

When he eventually took my advice and married Kim, we all went to the wedding. My daughter was a flower girl, wearing a twirly white dress, her hair piled high on her head and curled in the fanciest coiffure she'd ever worn in her four years of life. She looked like a little princess. I was in the wedding, too, reading a scripture passage they'd chosen. Being a part of their wedding felt like another part of the healing in our relationship.

These days, my brother and his wife live in Colorado and I live in Chicago. I wouldn't say we're super tight, but we care for each other. We don't talk that often, but when we do, we are honest and real with each other. We are reconciled, even if we are not best friends. If I hadn't listened to God and then to my brother, I think we would not have any relationship at all.

The ministry of reconciliation, which the Bible says God has given to us, begins with listening.

∿ The Power of Struggle ∿

Jesus said, "In this life, you will have trouble" (see John 16:33). Yet we always seem surprised by our struggles. The thing is, it is our struggles that really have the potential to unite us—to one another and to Jesus. Because right after Jesus mentions that life in this world is full of trouble, he adds, "But take heart! I have overcome the world." How has Jesus "overcome" the world? By forgiving us, by giving us the gift of life in a dying world. And this is not a gift we receive in isolation. We have other people, flawed as they may be.

When I listen to people talk about their struggles, when I come alongside them, when I suffer with them, I am embracing a truth: life is hard, but I am not alone in my pain. And they get to discover it too, if I am courageous enough to admit that I do not have it all together. Together, we receive the gifts Jesus has given us.

We often feel isolated by our difficulties. We think we are the only one who has doubts or difficulties, and they scare us. But when we listen to someone else who is struggling, we realize we're not the only one. Now, how do we find that kind of honesty? We only find it when we are willing to be that honest ourselves. When we risk truth telling, when we let go of image management, we find one another. Loving listening frees us from the isolation of struggling alone.

Author Alice Fryling says that as we grow in listening to God, others may ask us to be what she calls "a spiritual companion"—someone who helps others listen to God. This, too, takes us out of our isolation and can be an amazing gift, not only for the one who is listened to but for the listener as well. Fryling gives this wise advice for listening to others in spiritual companionship:

> Remember that in order to listen to another person in this way, we must be humble and respectful. I have found that this means "letting go" on my part. If I want to listen well, with love and awe, I need to let go of my need to be right. I need to let go of many preconceived opinions. I need to let go of my own self-consciousness and insecurities. And I need to let go of the need to appear wise, good, or even spiritual.[3]

If we are more concerned about appearing "wise, good, or even spiritual," than we are about actually listening to someone, we will end up isolated. When we are self-focused to the exclusion of others, we will push them away. They won't feel that we are hearing them; they will go looking for someone who can actually listen to their story and help them make sense of it. Listening is a gift that can bring us together.

"For where two or three come together in my name, there am I with them," Jesus told his disciples (Matthew 18:20). Listening to someone, especially someone whose pain has led them to a searching for God, is a way of "coming together." If we listen in the way Fryling describes, we create a space where the listener, speaker, and Jesus can get together. And when Jesus is there, then we really know we're not alone, and that is a gift of immeasurable worth.

∿ A One-Another Kind of Faith ∿

The Bible often gives directions about things we're to do "to one another"—as in, encourage one another, love one another, forgive one another, bear one another's burdens, admonish one another, be kind to one another.

Christianity, it seems to me, is a one-another kind of faith. That makes listening an essential part of it. You can't encourage without listening first. You can't bear one another's burdens unless you've listened to what those burdens are.

C. S. Lewis said true friendship often begins when we find someone to whom we can say, "What? You too? I thought I was the only one." That's a one-another kind of discovery.

We minister to others by listening, but when we listen, we also receive. We can, if we're open to it, hear God through others. In my experience, God hasn't spoken with a thunderous voice from the clouds, but he does sometimes give other people words to say that have pierced my heart, or comforted it. God heals us and cares for us through the words of others, if we are wise enough to heed them.

Sometimes this comes in the form of a sermon or lesson, but usually it comes when someone has listened to me and offered a question or observation, has reflected back what I'm saying, and it hits me in a new way.

Now, of course, not everything that other people say is a word from God, even when they claim it is. We have to be discerning. But often, the voice of love comes through the words of a friend who knows us and is praying for us. We need to listen.

We give and receive love by listening to others. We listen to their story and help them notice where God is at work. We can point out the growth we see in them; we can name their gifts and encourage them as they try to use those gifts to serve God.

When I listen to the pain and struggles of others, my listening can be an agent of healing both their pain and my own. And if I am open to it, when I patiently listen to the confessions of another, God will allow me to offer words that will help that person grieve their sin and then move forward toward restored relationship with God and others.

We're all ragamuffins, as Brennan Manning has said. No matter how good we are, we are *so* not God. But it seems to me that the Christian faith has not enough venues where we can readily admit this to one another. Or we may say, "Oh, I used to be a sinner, but now I'm really doing great!"

Well, I think all of us are in process and we have good days and bad days and, frankly, if we could all just admit this to each other, the Christian faith would be a lot more appealing to people who are wondering what it is all about.

Even the Apostle Paul, who certainly lived a God-focused life, wrote this: "For I have the desire to do what is good, but I cannot carry it out" (Romans 7:18). Read all of Romans if you want to look into the mind of a brilliant man who was honest about his struggles with sin.

Can you be real with others? If you can't, don't expect that others will feel safe admitting their struggles to you. You will miss out on the opportunity to grow by listening to others if you can't admit your own weaknesses. Can others be real with you, tell you what's really going on? How do you receive it when they do? Is vulnerability valued in your relationships?

∿ Listening from a Place of Weakness ∿

Now, I'm not talking indiscriminate dumping of all our psychological and emotional garbage on just anyone. That's not healthy or appropriate from either the giving or receiving end. Good listeners have clear boundaries. They are not emotional repositories for everyone else's problems. This is no easy line to tread. So, how can we listen lovingly but still maintain boundaries?

Perhaps you have a friend who seems very needy, who always looks to you to listen but never reciprocates. You dread the phone calls because you know it is going to be a one-sided conversation or that your friend will ask for another unreturned favor.

We all have seasons in certain friendships where we give more than we take. But is it a pattern in most of your friendships? Do you listen but not really speak truth to friends who may need it? Do you feel that people take advantage of you? Do you resent being taken advantage of but then slide quickly into feeling guilty about your resentment? Do you think it's "Christian" to *always* put others first?

It may be that you have a problem with setting boundaries, so you are listening from a place of weakness.

Loving listeners listen from a place of strength. They don't take on responsibility for things that are not their fault. They don't allow people to manipulate or blame or shirk responsibility.

I have tried to be a loving listener to my children. When my kids say, for example, "I'm bored," I listen. But I do not jump in and rescue or feel like I need to entertain them or fix the problem. I say, "Hmm, it sounds like you have a real problem. What do you think you are going to do about it?" They may not know at first. I tell them I think that must be a difficult problem, but I think they can figure out a solution, because they are wise and creative. I let them wrestle with it rather than jump in and fix, even though I am sympathetic. If they get desperate, I tell them one option is to clean the bathroom, if they so choose. Usually, that helps them come up with creative solutions. Now, I have to be willing to let them be creative, as long as they don't endanger themselves or others.

Yesterday—a warm summer day—their solution to having "nothing to do" was to ride their bikes to the corner drug store, where they purchased poster board with their own money. They each designed a poster, just for the fun of it. If I tell them to solve their problem I have to be willing to say yes to the bike ride and the spending of their allowances on what seemed a sort of odd project. But they enjoyed it and felt capable, not only in accomplishing their mission but in solving their own problems.

Listening from a place of strength means knowing when to affirm and when to challenge. I cannot always know these things on my own. I need discernment and wisdom. That's why it helps to invite God into the conversation. If we listen to others while listening to God, then we don't have to rely on our own strength, our own wisdom. We can pray that God will give it to us as we listen and speak.

If God is in the middle of our conversations, if we really listen to each other, we can build honest relationships where we share both our triumphs and our struggles, our joy and our pain.

Listening, prayer, and other practices will form me. If I continue to listen to others and to God, it will form my character. But it is not solely for myself, or even for God, that I undertake this journey of transformation. It is for the sake of others. God wants me to become more patient, loving, and kind. My growth is not just for the sake of my self-improvement but so that my actions toward others point them to faith, to Christ. And also, so that others can be comforted, healed, challenged.

My spiritual formation is not all about me. It's for those I live with, those I teach, even you who are reading these words. God is at work in my life to encourage you, to teach my children, to strengthen the body of Christ, that is, the Church. He's forming me so that my children have a loving mother. He's at work in your life to bless others. And when we engage in the practice of listening to each other, even in times of difficulty, we give God space to work, to form us.

Now, while God's work in my life is intended, in part, to help the body of Christ, that does not mean that I am supposed to fix people or that I am solely responsible for their spiritual development. When we listen very deeply, we realize that we cannot fix others. Only God can do that, and once I embrace and trust that God can handle that job, I am free to listen deeply and not worry about where God is going with this person. I can play my proper role, which is to listen and perhaps offer encouragement or truth, but leave the big picture to God. When we listen to others, we do it best if we are also listening to God at the same time.

There are spiritual practices that will help us tune in to God's voice, to train ourselves to listen. And so that is what we will explore next.

 Have you ever had another person speak God's word to you? Do you agree that the goal of community is to bring each other the message of salvation? Why or why not?

PART III

LISTENING PRACTICES

Listening is a spiritual practice. We've seen how listening to our lives and to others can create space for God, enabling us to hear him. It is also an essential element in other practices that lead us toward deeper connection with God.

By "spiritual practice," I mean those classical disciplines—prayer, reading scripture, solitude, self-examination, and others—that Christians have engaged in over the centuries to develop their relationship with God. These are not a means to impress God but, rather, specific activities we can do to increase space in our lives—sacred, God-focused space.

In this section, we'll look at just three practices: silence, reading scripture, and prayer. Each of these can be a chance for transformation. God has so much to offer us when we take the time to create some space through practice of these and other disciplines. But to receive it, we have to choose to listen, to focus on God rather than on the practice itself.

The goal is to open up space for God—a space where you can be with him, to really listen so that your life will be changed in ways you couldn't change it yourself. Listening puts aside our self-preoccupation and puts the focus where it should be—on God.

As you begin to engage in spiritual practices, you will want more than just ritual or obligation. You will desire an encounter; you will want it to somehow improve or at least deepen the rest of your life. If our focus is on God and on hearing him rather than on our own performance, this is much more likely to occur.

And to go the next step deeper requires that we not only listen for God but that we hear and, most importantly, respond. What does God want us to know, to be, to do? We must believe it, embrace it, engage in it. To be still and listen, then to act on what God has told us—that is what makes listening transformational.

All of our spiritual practices are transformed by listening. And our listening is transformed by the way we daily practice our faith. If we make a habit of giving, worshipping, offering hospitality and mercy, fasting, and other disciplines, not for the sake of legalism but in order to tune our ear to God's work in the world, we will hear him more clearly.

If we never read the Bible or meet with other believers, if we never take a step of faith to help someone else or give to the poor, we deny ourselves opportunities to grow, to be aware of what God is doing. These simple practices will tune our ear to what God is doing and inspire us to join in.

Still, just doing certain activities won't necessarily draw us into intimacy with the Father. I'm sure you've read the Bible sometimes and when you closed it, you couldn't remember what you read. You looked at the words and intellectually understood them, but you did not have, as Paul Tournier called it, a "personal encounter."

Perhaps you know of married couples who spend plenty of time in the same house but have little or no intimacy because they have lost the ability to really listen to each other. They may speak, yet they don't really listen or hear each other. They may exchange information about what's for dinner or what time the children need to be picked up from soccer practice or whether the electric bill was paid on time, but they don't go much deeper than that. Or they may argue, but their words are mostly words of blame rather than the sharing of feelings. Their relationship is not very intimate emotionally, even if it is occasionally intimate in a physical way.

In the same way, we may show up at church or a prayer meeting or even for our "quiet time" with God and be physically present but not emotionally or spiritually present. We may sing songs, read words, even follow along mentally as the pastor preaches, but we don't really listen in a transformational way. We may read the Bible or even talk to God, but we don't really hear what he says through either of these practices. Thus we walk away from the experience unchanged. Perhaps we're a little disappointed about that, or just resigned, thinking it would be impossible to be transformed by our church, our small group, our friends, our life—or even our God.

When we expect others to somehow "wow" us into change, to sweep us off our feet spiritually, to do something for us, we're likely to be disappointed. It is when we engage, when we really listen, when we participate in the process, that transformation begins.

Listening is not often included in traditional lists of spiritual practices, although spiritual direction is often referred to as "holy listening." But listening is an essential element of all spiritual practice and progress. Listening is what makes spiritual practices transformational rather than pharisaical: people who have a rules-and-regulations-based faith, who are worried about coloring inside the lines, who are prone to approach God with practices, rituals, whatever. The practice of listening takes the focus off of my input and puts it on God. It's not about the listening itself but, rather, whom I am listening to. If we focus on a practice, rather than on God, all we will accomplish is to become an expert at that practice. We won't give God the opportunity to change our hearts.

Jesus gave the Pharisees plenty of grief for the manner in which they engaged in spiritual practices. "Woe to you, teachers of the law and Pharisees, you hypocrites! You give a tenth of your spices—mint, dill and cumin. But you have neglected the more important matters of the law—justice, mercy and faithfulness" (Matthew 23:23). Jesus was aware that the Pharisees were more concerned with image management, with doing practices rather than allowing those practices to transform them. "On the outside, you appear to people as righteous but on the inside you are full of hypocrisy and wickedness," he tells the Pharisees in Matthew 23:28.

We often say, "Oh, those terrible Pharisees. I'm glad I'm not like them." Which, unfortunately, is exactly the same attitude Pharisees often had toward "sinners" (see Luke 18:9–14). Jesus' interactions with legalists of his day are recorded in scripture so we can be reminded that our tendency is to be *just like them.*

By exploring just three practices, my hope is that you will discover how to make any spiritual practice transformational by making deep listening a part of it.

CHAPTER VI

Listening in Silence

*Silence is one of the deepest Disciplines of the
Spirit simply because it puts the stopper on
all self-justification.*

—RICHARD FOSTER[1]

Driving down the expressway one day, I noticed a billboard for a wireless phone service. In bold letters it declared simply: "Silence Is Weird." The phone company's name was at the bottom of the sign in smaller letters. Don't be silent, the sign implored. Talk, communicate, keep in touch. Continuously. We'll give you a thousand minutes a month for just $39.99.

We live in a world where the most common adjective we put in front of silence is—"uncomfortable." As in, "There was an uncomfortable silence." We don't think of peaceful, tranquil, or soothing silence. Silence is uncomfortable. It's weird. We avoid it; we fill it with noise, with talking, with radio, television, or phone calls. We carry iPods so that our life has a soundtrack of our own design, so we can always have background noise. The radio is on all the time in the car or in the house. We have televisions in our kitchens so we don't have the opportunity to do simple chores like preparing food or washing dishes in quietness.

We're pretty sure we need a thousand minutes a month (plus more "free" minutes on nights and weekends) for talking on our cell phones alone. What if we spent a thousand minutes a month in silence? What would that look like? It's about 16.5 hours. Not counting the time you are sleeping, do you come anywhere near spending about 30 minutes a day in silence?

But what would be the point? Why spend time doing something that is so unproductive, so uncomfortable, so weird? Why?

Because if you let silence in, doing so will change your life.

Silence is simply pulling the plug on the noise. It is intimately linked to the practice of solitude. If we are to get away from the noise, we need to be alone. So this chapter will look at these two practices together. When we practice solitude and silence, we turn off the television, the radio. We get away from the kids, the office, the places where people have access to us and the ability to assault us with their needs and demands. In silence and solitude, we find freedom. God invites us to stop, to rest, to be quiet for a while and just listen to the voice of love.

Silence also requires that we let go of our own agenda. It is approaching God empty-handed, without a wish list, prayer, or even a Bible-study booklet. It is being with God for the purpose of simply focusing our attention. And that's where listening comes in.

Solitude and silence are traditional spiritual practices that, on their surface, are simply about withdrawing from people and noise in order to be alone with God. Many people meditate simply by being quiet and thinking of nothing or simply focusing on a word, such as *peace.* Others meditate on God as he reveals himself in nature. Spending time in silent meditation can be a helpful practice. But what happens when we enter into solitude and silence for the purpose of listening?

Engaging in spiritual disciplines is not a way of forcing God to show up and give us a "deep" experience. As I teach and lead retreats, I sometimes talk to people who are sad and frustrated with their attempts to practice solitude and silence. "I tried it," they say. "But nothing happened." As I listen to them, I become aware that they may have been silent, they may have been alone, but they are not sure why they were doing it. They did not really listen in the silence, perhaps because they did not realize that the listening is what makes solitude and silence transformational.

In the Christian tradition, solitude and silence were foundational practices. Jesus himself modeled these practices, and his followers have been using them as tools for creating space to listen to God ever since. In post-modern America, where silence is "weird," it's a bit harder to engage in this practice. But we need it more than ever because our world is so noisy and hurried.

Luke's gospel documents several instances of Jesus spending time in solitude, beginning with his extended time of solitude, fasting, and temptation in the desert for forty days (Luke 4:1–13).

Within the next three chapters, Luke notes three other instances of Jesus practicing solitude, sometimes for a short time, sometimes for a night: "At daybreak Jesus went out to a solitary place" (Luke 4:42); "But Jesus often withdrew to lonely places and prayed" (Luke 5:16); "One of those days Jesus went out into the hills to pray, and spent the night praying to God" (Luke 6:12).

Clearly, solitude was a regular practice, and usually it was a way for Jesus to pray and to listen to God—to pull away from and stop listening to the voices of others. In Luke 6, after spending the night praying, he chooses the twelve apostles. You have to assume that he and the Father had a conversation about this important decision.

It was also a place for him to listen to God when he might be tempted to listen to the voices of others. After the miraculous

> *Without silence there is no solitude. Though silence sometimes involves the absence of speech, it always involves the act of listening. Simply to refrain from talking, without an ear listening to God, is not silence.*
>
> —RICHARD FOSTER[2]

feeding of the five thousand, Jesus "dismissed the crowd. After he had dismissed them, he went up into the hills by himself to pray" (Matthew 14:23). He could have kept the crowd around and listened to their admiration. But he chose to be alone, to listen to God instead.

> *The practices of solitude and silence are radical because they challenge us on every level of our existence. They challenge us on the level of culture: there is little in Western culture that supports us in entering into what feels like unproductive time for being (beyond human effort) and listening (beyond human thought). They confront us on the level of our human relationships: they call us away from those relationships for a time so we can give undivided attention to God.*
>
> —RUTH BARTON[3]

Within the boundaries of solitude, we may simply be silent, still, waiting. Or we may read God's word, pray, meditate, engage in self-examination or confession. What we do depends, not on our whim or some sort of spiritual practice schedule but on what God calls us to. Even our decision about how to spend our time alone, then, begins with listening. We must remember that our desire or interest in solitude comes from a longing that God places in our hearts, whether we are aware of his authorship or not. When we move into solitude and silence, we have listened to that inner voice, and if we are wise, we will continue to make listening an essential part of our practice. However, this is not always easily done.

As Barton so compellingly explains, we are silent *so that* we can listen to God: being, listening, giving undivided attention to God—these are what make solitude and silence transformational.

And you may be protesting: "I have a quiet time every day. I log my thousand minutes a month, maybe more!"

Fair enough. But let me ask you this: How quiet are you in your quiet time?

For years I would have a "quiet time," with varying degrees of consistency. Ironically, I was rarely quiet during those times. I would read my Bible, which to me meant analyzing it, reading a commentary on it, or maybe trying to get my Bible-study homework done. I would study, try to memorize, work hard to simplify and reduce the text to what I thought it ought to mean, wrestle with difficult passages, and look for some way to explain or interpret them. My "quiet" time was filled with words—of scripture and about it, words in my journal, errant thoughts about other things. My quiet times also included a lot of spoken words. I would pray, dutifully following a prayer pattern of Adoration, Confession, Thanksgiving, and finally, *finally*, Supplication. Certainly, I learned things. There was value in the discipline, in the practice. I am not against using prayer patterns as a tool. As I prayed, I sometimes felt God was speaking to me, but this surprised me. Mostly, I didn't let the Spirit get a word in edgewise.

My dialog with God was more in the area of doing than speaking. I wanted God to do stuff for me more than I wanted to hear God speak into my life. It was as if I bargained like this: "I'll pray, I'll be a good girl, I'll serve at church, and you make things go well for me, you get me out of trouble, you bless my job, my relationships, my ministry. Sound good? Amen."

Listening to God requires that I let go of being so controlling in our relationship.

Through teachers, books, and mentors, I began to be more fully aware that prayer should be a two-way conversation. Oh, yeah, that's right, this is a relationship. I'd always known it in my head but conveniently forgot it whenever I prayed.

When I began listening during my quiet time, I was freed from feeling that I ought to read a whole chapter of the Bible at one sitting, or fill the blanks in a study guide, or say the right words to impress God or simply get noticed. When I listened before I spoke, when my prayer was "speak Lord, for your servant is listening" (1 Samuel 3:10), followed by actual quiet listening, things began to change: sometimes I was just a little bit aware of the Spirit's presence, of the *Paraclete* actually coming alongside; sometimes, there were not words from God but a feeling of love and acceptance; sometimes, for reasons I can't explain, tears came. Tears are a way that God speaks to us, if we will listen, if we will sit still long enough to figure out where those tears are coming from, if we will pay attention. Other times, I came face-to-face with the fact that on that particular day, I had to spend time in confession . . . and that was all. Or I simply had to acknowledge that I had a neediness that was beyond words.

∿ Silence in the Throne Room ∿

The Old Testament book of Habakkuk is only three short chapters, but it contains a valuable lesson about silence and listening. It begins with Habakkuk, a prophet, complaining to God at length. "How long, O Lord, must I call for help, but you do not listen? Or cry out to you 'violence!' but you do not save?" (Habakkuk 1:2). In other words, he prayed a lot like I often do, not in respectful silence but as if I were dropping angry notes in the suggestion box.

Thus begins a dialog between the prophet and God. God doesn't hold back, either. He denounces all manner of sin in an in-your-face reply. It ends with the oft-quoted verse, "But the Lord is in his holy temple; let all the earth be silent before him" (Habakkuk 2:20).

The third part of this short book is Habakkuk's prayer. His attitude has shifted 180 degrees. "Lord, I have heard of your fame; I stand in awe of your deeds, O Lord" (Habakkuk 3:2). He stops demanding that God listen to him and instead starts listening to God.

What brings about this shift, this change? Habakkuk listens to God, he realizes he's been a little presumptuous with the complaints, and, finally, he keeps silent before God.

Silence is an appropriate way to respond to the awesome power and strength of God. The Lord is in his holy temple, on the throne, in control. Sometimes we forget the power of that image. Instead, we focus on what the writer of Hebrews reminds us: Jesus can sympathize with our weakness. He came down off his throne to be with us, to become one of us. Therefore, the writer notes, "Let us then approach the throne of grace with confidence, so that we may receive mercy and find grace to help us in our time of need" (Hebrews 4:16).

Confidence, yes; arrogance, no. I have sometimes taken my accessibility to God for granted. I come jabbering into the throne room, thinking of the King as just my friend. He's a friend, yes, but not an equal. There is a reason why Jesus said to call him Father when we pray: he loves us; he's our daddy. But he's our Father, and our King, and deserves reverence. As I said earlier, he's not safe—that is, he's not predictable or controllable—but he's good. Our confident expectation that he will hear us is steeped in deep respect and willingness to hear him as well.

We sometimes have to regain an accurate picture of what that throne of grace looks like. This helps us appreciate what an astounding privilege it is to be able to walk right up to God and say, "Good morning, Dad."

Isaiah writes of a vision he has of God: "I saw the Lord, seated on a throne, high and exalted. And the train of his robe filled the temple" (Isaiah 6:1). He goes on to describe winged seraphs that attend him, continually singing, "Holy, holy, holy is the Lord God almighty; the whole earth is full of his glory" (Isaiah 6:3).

Isaiah is frightened and painfully aware of his imperfections in the presence of a perfect and holy God. He's not sure what to say. And yet God bids him to approach and to receive an assignment to be God's spokesman, his prophet. God promises that he will speak to Isaiah—and through him, if Isaiah is willing to listen.

When we approach God, it is often helpful to approach him by simply being quiet. Be still; breathe deeply. Slow down enough to imagine God, on his high and exalted throne, and then remind yourself that it is not just the King and Creator of the Universe who sits there in power and splendor, but that same person is also your loving Father. That's what is so astounding—that we can confidently approach such a person.

∼ Silence as a Balancing Weight ∼

Sometimes, our life circumstances call us into silence and solitude. This is a call that we are often tempted to resist. When I first started getting invitations to speak, I somehow managed to schedule three speaking gigs within two weeks. Some find such a schedule invigorating, but to me it felt overwhelming. I felt worried, wondering how I would find time to prepare. I had to teach about spiritual practices and was not sure if I would know what to say. The schedule, on top of my responsibilities with my young children, my writing, my housework and other chores, felt like a little more than I could manage.

Within a week, I talked to two different friends who both offered virtually the same counsel: "Be sure that you balance out all of that talking with some times of silence." Now, you'd think I'd have listened the first time. But I was reluctant. I had planned to spend time working with the words I would say, writing and rewriting my presentations. I had to fit in carpool driving and a PTA meeting as well. I didn't have time to just sit and be unproductive. I had a lot to get done! I figured I could spend time in solitude and silence after my busy weeks, not before. But when the second person said almost the same thing: spend time in silence, not just after the speaking but before, I thought perhaps God might be trying to tell me something. When two people who are more mature than you are offer you the same spiritual advice in the same week, it makes sense to pay attention.

When your life is weighed down, when the scales are out of balance because you are talking too much or there is too much noise around you, you need the balancing weight of silence. I didn't know I needed it then, but since I was learning about listening, I decided to try to pay attention.

So, even though it made me nervous, even though I was worried about being underprepared, I sat still. I set aside some time to put the phone ringer on silent and let the machine get it, to sit in a chair and look out the window at the trees in my backyard. I told God, here I am; you've called me, through the voices of wise friends, to be silent. And I listened. I breathed, slowly, for the first time in a while. I can't say I got some divine enlightenment, some radical insight. And I admit this was more than a little disappointing. I was hoping for words, some useful insights that I could mine for the talks I had to give. But as I sat in silence, listening, even though I didn't get a three-point outline for my talk, I was aware of God's presence. He was very much Emmanuel, God with me.

As a result of this practice, I was calmer, both at that moment and when I had to teach. I was able to be fully present when I taught. I realized that my demeanor with those I taught was more important than my words. People remarked on it, how peaceful I was, how simply present I was. Listening to God's call to silence, then listening in the silence, enabled me to invite others into spiritual practices that I had actually experienced rather than only studied about.

∿ Getting Alone ∿

In order to listen in solitude, we first need to practice solitude. This may seem obvious, but I often lament, *why doesn't God speak to me?* Why don't I get specific operating instructions, step-by-step directions? But when pressed, I must admit that I have not taken time to get alone, to actually even ask God's opinion, except over my shoulder as I run out the door.

 Solitude frees us, actually. . . . The normal course of day-to-day human interactions locks us into patterns of feeling, thought and action that are geared to a world set against God. Nothing but solitude can allow the development of a freedom from the ingrained behaviors that hinder our integration into God's order.

—DALLAS WILLARD[4]

I actually enjoy time alone, although it is hard for me to be still in that time. As a writer, I spend a lot of time by myself. It's a solitary vocation. After a day alone writing, with only the dog to talk to, I'm glad when my kids walk in the door, glad to be with them, to help them with their homework, to have their friends over to fill the house with joyful noise.

However, I have found that if I want to listen in solitude, my words must cease—both spoken and written. And I must intentionally withdraw from the noise around me, from the world that says, "silence is weird." Solitude may seem mysterious or inconvenient. How, exactly, is it done? Must we go to a retreat center or spend the weekend in a cloister?

In one word: no. Solitude is simply getting alone. It may only be for five minutes. Five minutes is better than nothing. In our world, finding even a few moments to be still is easier said than done. If you are the parent of small children, it may be intensely challenging. If you live alone or work in isolation, you may spend more time than you like in solitude already, and the idea of entering into it on purpose may seem illogical.

Could you possibly come away? Could you possibly follow Jesus, who the gospel writers seem to continually remind us, "often withdrew to lonely places and prayed" (Luke 5:16).

The solitude itself is the first step, though. Get out your calendar, your planner, your PDA, and find a block of time. This may feel somewhat mechanical. That's okay. How can you rearrange your schedule for even just a half hour of solitude each week? This will require you to make some trade-offs. Solitude, like other practices, requires us to say no to some things in order to say yes to God.

For example, if you decide to use part of your lunch hour to be alone with God, you will likely have to say no to lunch with your coworkers, or say no to working straight through your lunch hour, or no to going shopping. If you work from home, as I do, you may find it challenging to just sit and listen to God. I'm easily distracted by housework, chores, kids interrupting, phone calls. And my work is always there, even after the kids have gone to bed. It's tempting to just "finish up a few things" and end up spending too much time working and not enough just being still.

If your job is to parent small children, you may have to get a sitter for an hour or two to have time alone. In fact, if you are the parent of young children, forget having a long time with God every day. Take the moments you can grab, but once a week, have your husband or a friend watch your kids and take some time to just be quiet with God, to listen.

When she was single and in her twenties, my friend Gina began reading books like *Celebration of Discipline* by Richard Foster and *The Spirit of the Disciplines* by Dallas Willard. She began to explore spiritual practices and found that times of solitude were rejuvenating. She enjoyed spending time alone, whether it was for a few minutes during her lunch hour at work or for a weekend.

> *Let him who cannot be alone beware of community. Let him who is not in community beware of being alone. Along with the day of the Christian family fellowship together there goes the lonely day of the individual. This is as it should be. . . . The mark of solitude is silence, as speech is the mark of community. Silence and speech have the same inner correspondence and difference as do solitude and community. One does not exist without the other.*
>
> —DIETRICH BONHOEFFER[5]

Then she got married and had kids. Even one child made it hard to find time alone, so she set that aside for a while. But she found that she craved time with God. She wasn't sure how to make that happen as a mom. Their budget was tight. She took her daughter everywhere, almost never getting a sitter for anything.

"I couldn't justify it in my mind, to simply get away, especially spending money for a sitter," she said. "It was a struggle."

Gina talked with friends. Wisely, she let them counsel her about her need for solitude. She listened to not only their advice, but she also listened to, as she put it, "my desperation. I needed to be alone." When friends offered to watch her daughter while she spent time alone with God, she accepted their help.

Gina now has three young girls, but she's learned to take a time of solitude, a few hours a week. She hires a sitter or leaves the children with a friend and simply escapes. She leaves her house, with its phone, children, and other distractions, and goes to a coffee shop or park. She does not run errands, balance the checkbook, or make a shopping list. She might draw, or write in her journal, or read during that time. She prays, both speaking and listening to God. She returns to those practices that she learned before she had children and finds that they replenish her again, in new ways. She's learned that the way she lives with others is transformed by her ability to pull away from those she loves and cares for, to listen only to God.

Transformational solitude requires that you get away from people, noise, and distractions in order to listen to God. Without the listening part, you are simply alone and likely to focus on your own boredom, restlessness, or personal attempts to solve your problems.

∿ Take a Few Moments ∿

I make room in my schedule on a regular basis for solitude and silence, for the purpose of listening to God. Notice that I do this "on a regular basis." I don't manage it every day. But I don't beat myself up for that. Also notice that I don't say I *hope* to find room or even that I *try* to make room in my schedule. I make it. Now, each day is different. Sometimes I'm able to spend a good amount of time, sometimes very little. But I say no to other things in order to say yes to time alone with God. I manage it more often than not, because I know that just a few minutes of silence is better than none at all. I've learned I can be quiet in many places, in many different ways. I have found many new ways to be alone with God besides the traditional quiet time.

Some mornings, all I can manage is to stand in front of the coffee maker while it brews the first cup. I look out my east-facing kitchen window and look for the sun peeking through the thick trees of my backyard. I say, "Okay, Lord, here comes another day. Here I am, showing up for it." Then I just become quiet and try to get in touch with a little bit of gratitude for the fact that the earth is still spinning, that here comes the sun again, even if I can't see it through the clouds. God managed to keep the universe going without my help while I slept. It's just about two minutes, but it centers me, helps me get through the chores of the morning, and reminds me that God is with me all the time, and he's in control.

Some days, I get up early and sit and look out at the backyard, or sit in my garden if the weather is good. I love being in my garden, surrounded by herbs and flowers as I sit in a cracked plastic Adirondack chair that a neighbor had planned to throw away. I look at the dewy spider webs and listen to the birds, notice the roses and morning glories blooming. My family is inside, sometimes sleeping, sometimes just leaving Mommy alone because they know it is in their best interest. My time sitting outside (or by a window if it's winter) is always rejuvenating. But typically, it's not very profound.

Mostly, those few minutes alone give me time to simply notice what God has wrought in my garden, in my soul—to be still, to breathe, to listen. One summer morning, I sat in my garden chair and was quiet for quite a while. God brought impressions to mind. I noticed smells, sights, feelings. I just breathed it in. I tried to be present, not thinking about yesterday or my to-do list. After several minutes of stillness, I wrote this in my journal:

> The lilacs surround the garden, their scent invades the yard.
> I want the aroma of Christ to be as obvious in my life. The
> outer aroma comes from the inner reality, the roots and
> branches. The soil, the rain, the earth feeds the lilacs. What

feeds me? Silence feeds my soul. Flowers feed my soul. This rescued cast-off chair, where I can sit and feel the warm sun and smell lilacs and look at pansies. It all feeds my soul.

Writing in my journal is how I pray after I've been listening to God for a while. It's also how I notice, so that I will remember what God said, what he gave me.

Other days, the hustle of getting kids breakfast and packing lunches and quizzing them on their spelling words all at once makes it hard to get alone. One of the things that has helped me set aside time is something you'd think would keep me busier: we adopted a dog. Jack, a mutt cuter than most, is a fairly calm dog. But in the mornings, he is a seventy-five-pound bundle of energy. Part of this is my fault. He's come to expect a walk each morning.

He lies around, training those sad golden eyes on me as I get the kids ready for school. But then, as they get their shoes on, he gets a bit more energetic. Once I am dressed, he starts barking at me and wagging his tail. He practically knocks me down as I try to put on my sneakers. It's time for the walk! So every day, rain, snow, or shine, Jack and I go for our walk. We usually walk around a small pond a few blocks from the house. We walk for about a half hour, sometimes more if we run into some of Jack's doggie friends and he stops to play. But usually, I am just alone, wordlessly passing other walkers, joggers, and roller-bladers on the path by the pond. I notice the morning sky reflected on the pond, how the water looks different each day, depending on the wind and weather, while turning my attention to God as much as I can. As Jack runs and sniffs and takes care of business, I simply tell my Jesus, "Here I am, available. I love you. I'm listening."

As I walk alone, I sometimes pray. This can take various forms: listening prayer, or sometimes words of adoration or confession or just pouring out the pain I'm in at the moment. Sometimes I will reflect on a bit of scripture I'd read earlier in the morning or the day before. Sometimes I am just quiet, walking, looking at the trees, the sky, the pond. Sometimes, I'll pray a silent blessing on the joggers who whiz by or the old man fishing in the pond.

Last week on my walk, I came around the pond's west end and heard a loud honking flock from the sky, coming in from the southeast. Their white and tawny markings were black against the morning sky. They banked seemingly as one goose, announcing loudly their final approach. A floating seagull excused himself from the still pond, as the geese turned their wing flaps down and soared just inches above the water before landing. I listened to their collective sliding splash, like quiet timpani or polite applause. My prayer was simply one of gratitude, for the beauty I'd just seen and heard.

Over the weekend, my kids walked with me. I saw some geese approaching the pond and told my kids to listen. That same sound of their landing was all we heard together. My ten-year-old looked at me. "That is so cool," she said.

It's just a suburban retention pond, just a walk through the park. They are just geese, landing on that pond. But my experience of it is transformed by listening. And my listening is deepened when it is shared.

∿ More Than a Few Minutes ∿

These short times of solitude and silence, whether walking or standing in the kitchen, are helpful. But sometimes, I need more time to really slow down, to really listen deeply, to wait on God. So every few months I take a longer time of solitude. Sometimes I go to a park, sometimes to a retreat center. I try to spend at least half a day, sometimes a whole day. There's a small retreat house about an hour away. I love the name: Our Lady of the Angels. It's on the grounds of a monastery and Catholic school. It is absolutely nothing like anything I experienced in my evangelical upbringing, which is one reason I love it.

One day I went there, checking in when I arrived with the nun who runs the house and who offers spiritual direction if you so desire. I didn't. I only wanted silence and solitude, time to sort some things out. The house is small, but the property is huge. There are gardens, fields, and woods to walk through. There was so much that God and I talked about that day, all because I was away from distractions of my regular life, although I spent the first hour fighting those distractions. I eventually wrote them down in my journal, just to get them out of my mind. This worked all right, but for a while I still vacillated between fatigue and having imaginary arguments with several people I was angry with, including God, who seemed to be slacking off on handling my priorities, especially on intervening and setting these people straight. All these complaints, all of my whole self, I brought to this day. Meet me, I prayed. It was almost like a dare.

The house had a little porch, and I spent part of the morning just sitting, letting myself get quiet, watching cottonwood fluff fall. There must have been a million cottonwood trees on that property, and all of them were releasing their white fluffy seeds at once. It was profuse, like a snowstorm. It brought to mind the verse: "though your sins be as scarlet, they shall be as white as snow" (Isaiah 1:18). I looked up the verse and noticed that God prefaces this promise to white-out my sins with a simple request: "Come, let us reason together." It was his invitation to me that day, almost daring me back. Don't just get away, the Spirit seemed to be saying. Get away so that you can listen. So we can dialog.

During the day, I walked through fields, I prayed. I wrestled with the temptation to make phone calls. I took a nap. I read a little scripture and a little Henri Nouwen. I looked at flowers, trees, a statue of Mary in a beautiful grotto. I moved slowly, noticing

God, just being quiet. I wrote down some goals, some desires for my career and ministry, trying to listen to God as best I could as I wrote.

One of the most significant moments of the day came in late afternoon as I walked a path, along which were elaborate stone carvings of the Stations of the Cross. Each scene, in relief, was hewn from one side of a geode-filled, moss-covered boulder, like those Easter eggs with one side removed and little scenes in them. I slowly walked the stations, stopping to meditate on each one.

As I stood silent and helplessly watched Christ stumbling on the Via Dolorosa, I asked him, "Why? Why did you keep going? Why didn't you call legions of angels, strike dead your accusers, just give up, whatever?"

I stood, feeling the silence, listening to the wind singing in the tall oaks over my head, not even really expecting a reply. In the quiet, Jesus answered me. "So that I could be here with you today," he whispered in my heart. "That's why." I sat by a quiet pond near the carvings and wept.

∽ Not Going There ∽

Perhaps as you read about my experiences of solitude, you are saying, "Well, I can't do solitude. I hate being outside; I'm just not a nature-lover. And I don't like being alone."

That's okay. I happen to have had some significant experiences of God in outdoor settings. That's my thing. You may choose another location. You can be alone in a library, an art museum, your house. God has created each of us uniquely. Some of us connect with him through his creation. Others experience God most deeply when they worship or when they study, others when they are helping others or serving in some way. Listen to your life; pay attention to how God made you. Incorporate that, if possible, into your solitude experiences.

For example, if you love to listen to music, then start a time of solitude by listening to a worship tape. Dance around to it if you like; worship God with your body, if that feels helpful. Then turn the music off, settle yourself down, and simply reflect in silence on what you have heard, on how God stirred your heart. Be wherever it is that the music took you. Linger in that place. There is no one "right" way to engage in this practice, except that you must be alone and quiet.

The trouble is, as soon as you sit and become quiet, you think, Oh, I forgot this. I should call my friend. Later on I'm going to see him. Your inner life is like a banana tree filled with monkeys jumping up and down. It's not easy to sit and trust that in solitude God will speak to you—not as a magical voice but that he will let you know something gradually over the years.

—HENRI NOUWEN[6]

For some, that in itself is a huge hurdle. "I can't do solitude. I'm just not wired up that way," said one woman I was mentoring. "God made me a very relational person."

If you are a relational person, if you love being in groups, if you feel God's presence when you are with people, that's who you are. Yes, God made you that way and often speaks to you through others. But God also wants to be enough for you, at least some of the time. If you are very extroverted, you might be tempted to rely on others for your spiritual growth. Even though it is a stretch, solitude is an essential practice for you. If you love to talk, silence is a necessary discipline.

Sometimes, we say we can't do solitude because we are simply afraid of it. Just being alone is frightening enough but to actually be alone for the purpose of listening? That's even more terrifying. You may say, well, God doesn't speak to me like that. Really? Have you ever given him the chance to do it? Have you ever just been still and silent for more than a few minutes? Or is silence too weird, too uncomfortable, for you?

Fear of solitude and silence is normal. After all, it's not what we typically do. Our fear may stem from any number of things. Perhaps we're scared that God won't show up. Perhaps we're afraid that he *will* show up and demand more of us than we're capable of giving.

What scares you about solitude? What fear keeps you from trying it or keeps you at a level where you spend time alone but don't listen in that time?

"The willingness to name our fear as we enter into solitude opens the way for God to reassure us with his presence," writes Ruth Barton. "It also enables us—eventually—to peel back the fear, revealing something even truer: our desire for God. This desire is the flip side of our fear."[7]

Fear shuts out; desire invites in. Listen to the voice of your desire. Talk to God about your fears as you move into the practice of solitude; be honest about your resistance. Then listen for his reassurances. Stay with the fear or uncertainty long enough, and you'll begin to see that it really is the "flip side" of your fear.

∿ Practicing Silence ∿

Silence and solitude are linked. Yet you can be alone and not be quiet. You can be silent but not alone. But when we intentionally withdraw from people and from the noise of the world, we are able to pray, to simply be with God and, hopefully, to listen to him. Silence and solitude enhance each other, especially when they are practiced together, not just for their own sake but for the purpose of listening to God.

Other times, we can practice silence in our everyday life. Even when we are with people, we can offer them our presence without words, or with few words. Sometimes we find ourselves alone, in the car, in the house. There's a temptation, sometimes, to run from solitude, to invite anyone, even Oprah or Rush Limbaugh, to be with us so we won't have to be silent, we won't have to be alone. But don't flip on the TV or the radio the minute you walk in the house, using it as a backdrop of noise. Leave it off. Let there be silence, even if it's only once in a while.

Try turning off the radio when you are driving in your car, especially if you are driving alone. Pray as you drive. Imagine Jesus is in the passenger seat. Do you drive any differently? Listen to what that might mean, about what might need to change in your actions and attitudes.

When I am doing chores around the house, I will sometimes put on music. My musical tastes are widely varied and attached to mood: sometimes I'll put on Fernando Ortega worship music, sometimes some sort of Celtic thing that stirs my ancestral soul, sometimes jazz, or if I'm feeling old and nostalgic, Simon and Garfunkel.

But other times, I will practice silence when I'm cooking or cleaning or doing laundry. I will fold, stir, wash, or scrub in silence. One winter day, I washed the dishes in silence. I don't like doing dishes because it seems just as I finish them there's another pile of pots and pans dirtied and waiting on the counter. But as I made myself just tackle the chore, I worked quietly. I looked out the window over the sink at my backyard. I may have complained in my head; I may have started out musing over all the things I had to do to get ready for Christmas, not the least of which was doing the dishes every day. God spoke to me in the midst of it, about the privilege of my little suburban life, with its hot and cold running water, central heat, and plenty of food to get those dishes dirty. I later wrote a poem about the experience:

Long tree shadows soldier
Across the snow dusty lawn.
Blue sky belies the cold.
At kitchen sink,
Hands in warm, soapy water
I think—what a false blue,
False sun, watched through window
Steamed by hot dishwater. I
Swirl the dishrag and listen,
Looking for truth
In a mundane chore.
And it is, of course, this:
'Tis a gift to have warm water
and a steamed window to peer through
on this December afternoon.
I look at my warm, wet hands
Sleeves rolled up
And breathe a prayer of thanks.

 Do you practice listening silence? If so, what is that like for you? If not, what keeps you from doing so?

Do you agree that solitude brings freedom? How does it align us with God?

How do you feel about spending time engaged in silence? Does it bother you to have what feels like "unproductive" time? What would be the purpose of doing that?

What do you think Bonhoeffer means when he says to "beware" of being alone or in community? Which do you prefer, solitude or community? How much time do you spend in each?

Have you experienced the "monkeys jumping up and down" in your mind when you try to spend time in solitude? How are solitude and trust related?

CHAPTER VII

Listening to Scripture

Then a cloud appeared and enveloped them,
and a voice came from the cloud:
"This is my Son, whom I love. Listen to him!"
—MARK 9:7

I have made my way in the world with words. From my child-hood, which was lined with books, to my adolescent journals and mournful (now laughable) songwriting attempts, to my career as newspaper reporter, freelance writer, and, eventually, author, I have loved words and their power. While I appreciate music, art, dance, and other creative expressions, for me there is nothing more beautiful than the perfectly turned phrase.

Even as a child, my love for words drew me to the Word, the *Logos.* I loved reading and hearing Bible stories. I loved the myste-rious riddle that the Word of God (the Bible) was about the Word of God (Jesus). John—the disciple some argue was Jesus' closest friend on earth—writes this about the one he loves: "In the begin-ning was the Word. And the Word was with God. And the Word was God. And the Word became flesh and lived for a while among us" (John 1:1–14).

Or, as Eugene Peterson paraphrases, "The Word became flesh and blood, and moved into the neighborhood."[1] What does that mean? It means the author steps into the story for a while to speak truth and demonstrate what he meant—to clear things up,

This Word is a Word that is involved in human existence. It is not some sort of static concept. In New Testament times the prevailing philosophy of the age, Stoicism, had a concept of logos or "word" as the shaping, organizing, forming principle of the universe that held everything together and directed its course; but it was a very impersonal, uninvolved kind of word. The Word we are speaking of is a Word that is actively involved in human existence. Here is one of those dimensions of the incarnation so important for us to grasp: not simply the idea of God's becoming human (not that we should lose that) but that the Word of God is intimately and vitally involved with us in the midst of life.

—ROBERT M. MULHOLLAND[2]

it seems—to speak out loud, to tell stories, to really connect with the people he had been trying to speak to and claim as his own for generations.

For a while, God's word was not just written, not just an oral tradition, not just a story—it was among us, in the form of a poor rabbi in a tiny country in the Middle East. He spoke provocative words to the people around him, trying to tell them about God's kingdom and using stories of everyday things to show them what it was like (a mustard seed, a bit of yeast, a woman who had lost a coin). But God's word is more than Jesus, more than his stories.

This is why the story of your life is so important, why stories in general are essential, why Jesus himself taught with stories, rather than just profound ideas. There is power in story.

That's why so much of the Bible is story—to get our attention, to plow the hard soil of our souls so we can receive the little seeds of truth God wants to plant.

As a writer, I often find myself walking the aisles of, say, my local Barnes & Noble, or surfing amazon.com with a kind of quiet desperation: What can I say that has not been said before? The truth is, there really is nothing new under the sun, except the stories that God has given me to tell.

Other people may have observed the same principles I write about; they've had the same points in their outline. But no one has lived my story. Or anyone else's story. God intersects human history, not just in the Incarnation but in daily incarnations, in our individual histories.

I often use interviews as a research technique, because when you can capture someone's story, it's often a clearer kind of truth than facts alone. Because clear, compelling stories connect us, speak to us. That's why, I think, the Bible is full of stories. Because God has something to say, and he knew we'd get it better if he used stories.

But how do I know when it's God? How can I recognize him in my story? How can I recognize his voice? Reading the Bible helps. Its

 The disciples came up and asked, "Why do you tell stories?"

He replied, "You've been given insight into God's kingdom. You know how it works. Not everybody has this gift, this insight: it hasn't been given to them. Whenever someone has a ready heart for this, the insights and understandings flow freely. But if there is no readiness, any trace of receptivity soon disappears. That's why I tell stories: to create readiness, to nudge people toward receptive insight. In their present state they can stare till doomsday and not see it, listen till they're blue in the face and not get it."

—MATTHEW 13:10–13,
THE MESSAGE

poetry paints a picture of God. Its stories shed light on the mystery that he is. Reading the Bible acquaints you, not only with God's actions and personality but with his voice.

If you know the type of things that Jesus would say by making yourself familiar with the story of his life on earth (as recorded in Matthew, Mark, Luke, and John), you'll be better able to decide if that little voice in your head is his, yours, or someone else's. If you have read the Old Testament prophets, who mouthed words from God like, "I have loved you with an everlasting love," then you might be more likely to realize that he's still saying that to you. You're less likely to be deceived into thinking that the voice of shame somehow comes from God. You will know that it certainly is not from God, because God doesn't talk like that. A voice of correction, or sorrow over our sin, perhaps. But not a voice of shame.

Without knowing God through his word, which Walter Wangerin calls "God's dictionary," we may not recognize or comprehend his language. "To recognize the word of God in our own lives, then, it behooves us to know his language as recorded in the Bible. We must learn Scripture in order to distinguish God's voice from, say, the voices of our own yearnings!"[3]

The word, should we hear and heed it, is active, or more accurately, interactive. It is God in us working for a purpose beyond ourselves. It is God inviting us to listen and participate in not just our own story but his story as well.

What does the Bible say about itself? The overall theme seems to be: don't just read but live it out. Listening to God through the scriptures seems to involve not just hearing but doing.

"For it is not those who hear the law who are righteous in God's sight, but it is those who obey the law who will be declared righteous" (Romans 2:13). Now, well-meaning people may disagree on what actions constitute obedience, but if we're reading just to observe and notice but not to actually do anything, what's the point?

The Bible offers some insight on listening that I think is helpful:

> Do not merely listen to the word, and so deceive yourselves. Do what it says. Anyone who listens to the word but does not do what it says is like a man who looks at his face in a mirror and, after looking at himself, goes away and immediately forgets what he looks like. But the man who looks intently into the perfect law that gives freedom, and continues to do this, not forgetting what he has heard, but doing it—he will be blessed in what he does [James 1:22–25].

Listening means "looking intently into the perfect law that gives freedom." We don't take it casually. And we see that it gives us not just rules and restrictions but freedom.

But how do we listen to the Word? And not just as passive observers but as active listeners who then act on what we hear, so that the Word might continue to be "fleshed out" by our acts of love? Where is the Word in each of our stories, in our daily lives? How do we look intently into the Word?

When we listen to God's Word, we listen to Jesus, not just what he said two thousand years ago but what he continues to say to us. His truth comes through our lives and through others, as we've already explored. But it also comes through this amazing book, the Bible.

∿ Engage Your Mind ∿

To really listen to scripture requires us to engage both our mind and our heart. "Be transformed by the renewing of your mind," Paul wrote in Romans 12:2. That is to say—the renewing of your mind, *not* the entrenching of it. "To renew" means to challenge the status quo, to make things new, to refresh or change. What new thing is God doing? What assumptions can the Spirit be challenging through the Word?

Reading, studying, and reflecting on scripture is a foundational Christian practice. What we read and reflect on shapes our beliefs and our practices. Our thoughts influence our actions. Throughout history, people have often taken writings of great thinkers or even not-so-great thinkers and reflected on them. And this, for better or for worse, shapes who they are and what they do.

If we say we are going to live out the teachings of Christ, or anyone else, we need to read, study, and reflect on those teachings—in other words, to engage our mind as we read and listen.

I grew up in a church that taught me the importance of memorizing scripture. As an adult, I'm thankful for that because there are so many times in my life when I have prayed and tried to listen to God, and words of scripture will come up on the Power-Point screen of my brain. If you've listened enough to scripture, it's there in your subconscious, and God can pull it up and whisper it to you, and you know it's God because it's the words you recognize as his.

The verses, even if I can't always recite them word-for-word precisely, are hidden in my heart. They can't help but influence my decisions or actions. There have been times I may have chosen to disobey, but I know what is right.

Even if you did not grow up with such a legacy, God can speak to you through scripture. You can learn to listen to God's word. But in order to do so, you've got to read it.

When I learned Bible verses as a child and teenager, I wasn't told to meditate on those words. But if you memorize something, you *do* meditate on it. And if you meditate long enough, you *will* memorize. If your focus is on the truth of the words, on what God is saying to you through them rather than the effort of memorization, you are likely to end up being able to remember them.

Knowing the scriptures can guard us against putting words in God's mouth. What God is telling us and what we want God to say can sometimes be two different things. If we listen to the Bible, we'll recognize God's voice among the many that shout for our attention.

If we spend time listening to MTV or reading *People* magazine, that's what we are meditating on, even if we don't think of it as meditating. If we repeatedly hear something, our mind will retain it. Think of how many song lyrics you've memorized, simply by hearing songs on the radio. Meditation begins with repetition, to think about something, even on a subconscious level. And that is what will shape our souls and thoughts, even our actions.

 Meditation is not meant to be esoteric or spooky or reserved for gurus reciting mantras in the lotus position. It merely implies sustained attention. It is built around this simple principle: "What the mind repeats, it retains."

—JOHN ORTBERG[4]

What we focus on and think about, even passively, affects us. Ultimately, it forms us. I find it hard to be intentional about what I listen to and watch. We can be bombarded by images that are attempting to sway our opinion, tell us what to buy . . . or what to at least lust after. Without even trying or realizing it, I will begin to believe that the advertisements are true, and I really do need certain clothes or makeup to be okay. I will begin to believe that certain moral choices really aren't all that bad. I don't mean to think this way. It's just that if I meditate on certain things on television or in fashion magazines, that's what shapes my mind and my ideas.

Listening intentionally requires that we focus our minds, that we be mindful about what we read and reflect on. It transforms the practice of simply reading when we listen to what any given text might be saying to us personally.

Engaging our mind with the truth of the Bible provides a foundation. It is an important part of listening to God. But I've found that if I "stay in my head" and just remain a detached observer of truth, it doesn't really change me. In order to be transformed, I need to let truth seep down from my head to my heart.

Our view of God is colored by our experience, what people we respect have told us. And our view of God, however distorted it may be by our woundedness, colors our view of scripture. To some extent, we often find in scripture what we already "know"—that is, we bring our bias to it. So how can we overcome this tendency to bring our own preconceived notions to the Bible? I think the key is to learn to listen not only with our mind but also with our heart.

∿ Open Your Heart ∿

We sometimes give less value in our culture to the heart, but in the Bible the heart was not something sloppy, sentimental, or irrational. It was the essence of personhood—the place where your true self lived and made decisions. It encompassed not only emotions but a person's will and decision-making capacities.

Psalm 119:11 says, "I have hidden your word in my heart that I might not sin against you." We don't memorize for memory's sake or to earn gold stars. We don't do it to *win,* despite the not-so-subtle messages of my childhood. We do it to battle against sin, or at least to struggle mightily against it. Sometimes when I question or doubt or am faced with a decision and ask for guidance, God will bring to my mind one of those verses that I memorized as a child. It's a way God guides, illumines, encourages me to choose good.

Hearts like ours, which may have been wounded or even broken, don't always open quickly.

It is very hard to listen in a hurry. This is especially true when it comes to reading, studying, and reflecting on scripture.

The single biggest barrier to listening to scripture (or really, listening to anything) in our day is simply the pace of our lives. We are moving too fast. You cannot meditate in a hurry. To listen to scripture, we have to read slowly, letting things sink in, pondering them.

I'm sure you've had the experience of reading something (this is typical with textbooks) and then, a few seconds later, not remembering what you read. You read, but you did not retain what you read. In other words, you didn't really listen to the text.

Listening to scripture involves more than just reading. We must study and comprehend, but this doesn't necessarily allow us to listen. Sometimes we bring so much of our own thoughts, baggage, our own desire for what we want the Bible to say, that it's as if we are trying to get the Bible to listen to us. We're using it to prove a point or justify our actions, or, sometimes, to try to manipulate others.

 The seed cast on good earth is the person who hears and takes in the News, and then produces a harvest beyond his wildest dreams.

—JESUS, QUOTED IN MATTHEW 13:23, *THE MESSAGE*[5]

Robert Mulholland, in his book *Shaped by the Word,* distinguishes between two types of reading: *informational,* in which we quickly gather the basic facts (we're controlling, or mastering the text) and *formational,* in which we slowly read for deeper meaning, letting go of the need to control and allowing what we read to sink in enough to change our minds and hearts.

. . . Allow the text to master you. In reading the Bible, this
means we come to the text with an openness to hear, to
receive, to respond, to be a servant of the Word rather than
a master of the text. Such openness requires an abandonment of the false self and its habitual temptation to control
the text for its own purposes.[6]

What would it look like to let the Bible speak, to let the text
master me, to listen to it and see what God wanted to say, without
bringing my agenda to my reading? It sounds a bit dangerous,
actually. And very unfamiliar.

Growing up evangelical, I worked very hard to be "a master
of the text" via study and memorization. I didn't get much training in listening or contemplative reading. Preachers sometimes said
they had a "word from God," but mostly, the word we got from
God was one we already had, bound in leather. I was supposed to
memorize and master the text. I had no clue what it would look
like to let the text master *me.*

The Bible was all true, they told me, and the key to the reli-
gion I grew up with was to memorize and study it. Study the
Bible. That's what we did. We learned all about it, memorized it,
came up with ways to attempt to apply it to our lives (which we
may or may not have actually *done,* but at least we knew what the
application points were!).

We had a song we sang often at Sunday school: "The B-I-B-
L-E, yes that's the book for me! I stand alone on the Word of God,
the B-I-B-L-E!"

I'm grateful for wonderfully creative teachers who simply
told me the stories of the Bible and found ways to make memorizing fun. Well, maybe not fun, but at least loud and rowdy. (Picture twenty first-graders shouting out "Genesis! Exodus!
Leviticus!" at the top of their lungs.) As a result, by the time I was
about eight years old, I knew most of the Bible's stories and had

memorized the books of the Bible (both testaments) and countless verses.

On the downside, I had a rather militaristic view of the whole thing, what with Bible "drills" and contests to see who could memorize the most verses. Apparently, the Bible was something you could use to win. I liked to win. I used it to win not only Bible drills but also the approval of my teachers, my parents, even, to a certain extent, my peers.

That's not to say I didn't apply it at all. I tried very hard to be a good girl, to obey the rules. But did the Bible transform me? I don't know. Maybe. Did I really listen to its wisdom, deeply? Even then, I loved words, and I loved reading the Bible. I especially liked the poetry of the Psalms and the pithy wisdom of Proverbs.

I suppose I was shaped by those words, as well as the stories I read and heard and saw illustrated on a flannel-graph board. What I came away with was that God loved words the way that I did and also that God loved me. I was confident in that—that God was a loving light, a friend, not a fierce or angry judge. I think I have my parents to thank for that, as well as my Sunday school teachers. For that, I'm again extremely grateful.

The downside of knowing the Bible so well as a child is that, like anything very familiar, you can begin to take it for granted. Several years ago, I was in a place where I read my Bible mostly out of obligation. I felt like I had read it all before, studied it, even led studies about much of it. It felt sort of, I don't know, old.

But to really listen to God through scripture, I had to learn to listen. I wasn't sure exactly how to do that. When I was introduced to the ancient practice of *Lectio Divina,* everything changed.

The Latin words *Lectio Divina* mean "Divine Word." There are various forms of this method, but the common ground they share is this: read a short passage slowly, several times, and listen for God to speak to you personally through it. You spend lots of time just being silent, waiting for God to speak through the text, to your heart. It's a simple method that will allow you to try "formational reading" or "spiritual reading" that lets you listen to the text, lets it speak to you. For those of us who grew up studying the Bible, this is a stretch at first, because we have to surrender some of the control. We have to really listen.

You can read the Bible on your own this way, but here's how I experienced it in a group setting. The leader read a short passage of scripture; I believe it was the passage in Matthew that describes Jesus walking on water and Peter getting out of the boat. She asked us to listen for the word that seemed to jump out at us from the text. We went around the circle and had each person just say the single word that they "heard" without any comment. Then we were silent.

Then she read the same passage again, and again listened for a word that stood out to us. This time, though, we were asked to share, if we knew, just a sentence or two about what it was we thought God wanted us to *know*. What was he saying to us, personally? We went around the circle, and even those of us who had heard the same "word" found that God was saying different things to each of us with that word. For example, for some, the word "afraid" stood out; for others, it was Jesus' command to Peter: "come." But our reasons, our understanding of what God was saying to us through that word, was deeply personal and different for each of us.

Finally, the leader read the text one last time and, after a time of silence, asked us to share what, if anything, we felt God was asking us to do as a result of the word we'd heard and what he wanted us to know. Again, the text spoke to each of us in a unique and personal way.

For me, I believe it was the word "afraid." It's in the passage twice, when Jesus says, "don't be afraid" and when Peter sees the wind and waves and is afraid.

I knew God was calling me to a new season of ministry, but I was scared. I didn't want to risk it, because I was afraid of what it would change in me, in my marriage, in other relationships, in my responsibilities. I was also afraid of failing. But as I listened to God through scripture that day, he clearly told me, "Don't be afraid."

Now, there are still times I get scared. But rather than just look at the Bible and say, "It says we shouldn't be afraid," I can look at that passage and say, "Here's where God said, Keri, don't be afraid." It wasn't just his Word; I mean, it wasn't just something that was true but objective, separate from my experience. It was his word to me, his interaction with me, something I needed to not only know but also to act on.

You can read scripture this way in a group or on your own. You can learn more about this practice in much more detail from reading other books, including some I've quoted in this chapter (*Soul Feast* by Marjorie Thompson explains it in much greater detail). But the point is not just to learn *about* this practice but to *practice* this practice. Read the Bible slowly, as if you were reading a love letter, as if it were God's word directly and personally to you, which of course it is.

These days, I lead other people through *Lectio Divina*. I teach people how to meditate on scripture. It's something I would have been

Spiritual reading is reflective and prayerful. It is concerned not with speed or volume but with depth and receptivity. That is because the purpose of spiritual reading is to open ourselves to how God may be speaking to us in and through any particular text. . . .
Spiritual reading is a meditative approach to the written word. It requires unhurried time and an open heart. If the purpose of our reading is to be addressed by God, we will need to practice attentive listening *[emphasis mine] and a willingness to respond to what we hear.*

—MARJORIE THOMPSON[7]

afraid to do, had I listened to my insecurities or even other people, instead of listening to God. I'm grateful that the Bible is not just a good word, but it's God's Word, to me personally. I don't know about you, but I need a God like that.

∿ Let the Word Dwell ∿

We do not listen to God in a vacuum but rather in the context of our lives. The spiritual disciplines we've looked at individually are completely intertwined.

Colossians 3:16 says, "Let the word of Christ dwell in you richly as you teach and admonish one another with all wisdom, and as you sing psalms, hymns, and spiritual songs with gratitude in your hearts to God."

What would it look like to let the Word dwell richly in my life? To soak into the fibers of my being? From this verse, it looks like Christ's dwelling in me is not for my sake but for others. God gives us the Word, and words, to share with others. Here's an example of how several kinds of listening came together for me recently:

I called one of my closest friends one morning. "How are you doing?" I asked her. I knew she was pretty stressed: she and her husband were having an addition built on their house, and the ensuing chaos and inevitable problems and countless decisions that needed to be made were wearing on her.

"Actually, I'm not doing very well," she replied, and I could hear in her voice that she was answering me with a restrained honesty. "Could you come over?"

So I did. There were other things I had to get done that day, but they could wait. It seemed very clear to me that God wanted me to go.

As I drove to her house, I wondered what I could say. I prayed for wisdom. But God just seemed to be saying: simply listen to her. Do not solve, do not attempt to fix or medicate or distract. Simply be with her and listen deeply, listen as empathetically as you can.

Frankly, this was a relief. I didn't have any words of wisdom, but I didn't need any. I just needed to listen and say things like, "That must be so hard" or "I know you're hurting and I'm sorry." It was also disconcerting. There's a bit of dysfunction in me that really believes, despite years of evidence to the contrary, that I can fix people, solve their problems, or at least give them some profound advice.

My friend poured out her heart to me that morning. The building project was just the tip of the iceberg; there was so much in her heart that was hurting. I simply sat with her, listening, letting her cry, trying to understand. I resisted any urge to give advice, which was actually not that hard because I had no clue what would resolve these things for her, no remedy for her pain. I ignored my little "fix it" voice, knowing it was much weaker than it was pretending to be. I tried to simply be with her, so she would not have to be alone in a painful place.

As I left her house, I promised to pray for her, although I wasn't sure what to pray for.

The next day, I was reading my Bible. I try to make a habit of reading slowly through one book of the Bible at a time, going forward only after reading each section for several days.

I was reading in Luke 5. It tells of Jesus speaking to the Pharisees and teachers. The house is crowded; no one can even get in the door. Outside, a few men are carrying a friend on a mat. He's paralyzed, so he couldn't get to Jesus by himself, even if the way were clear. But his friends believe Jesus can heal their friend, and they are desperate for him to do so—so desperate that they go up to the roof, rip a hole through it, and lower their friend (who may have been a bit embarrassed by the whole thing) into the house. Luke tells us "they went up on the roof and lowered him on his mat through the tiles into the middle of the crowd, right in front of Jesus" (Luke 5:19).

Jesus doesn't seem to miss a beat or be bothered in the least by the intrusion. Luke notes, "When Jesus saw their faith, he said, 'Friend, your sins are forgiven'" (Luke 5:20). The story goes on to tell of the man's healing. (Although for a few moments, interestingly, he is forgiven, but still lying on the floor. His heart is healed, but he's still not walking, because Jesus gets into a bit of tiff with the Pharisees for claiming he can forgive sin.)

I read the story, which is told in just ten verses, several times. I listened for which word or phrase stood out. Each time, the phrase "right in front of Jesus" seemed to jump from the page.

I sat quietly in my chair by the window, where I visit with God most mornings. I pondered the meaning. "Jesus, I want to be right in front of you, I want to keep you ever before me," I prayed. What would I have to do to stay right in front of Jesus? I wasn't sure. It wasn't fully clear to me why this phrase had stood out. I thought it probably had something to do with me, with my life and putting it at Jesus' feet.

I sat quietly for a little while longer. Then the kids came down for breakfast. We made their lunches; I signed their homework, helped them find jackets and backpacks, and all the other tasks involved in getting them off to school. After they left, I dressed and took the dog for our morning walk.

I walked around the pond in the park and continued to pray. I thought again of God's word to me: "right in front of Jesus." I was quiet, just walking, enjoying the sky and trees, simply turning the phrase over in my mind, not really pushing for meaning but trying to remain open.

And then, like sunlight breaking through the clouds, it hit me. It wasn't *myself* I needed to put "right in front of Jesus." It was my friend, who was paralyzed by the pain and chaos of her life—the friend I'd cried with and listened to the day before. She was stuck, immobilized, and needed some friends to carry her to Jesus and ask for her healing.

I was a little embarrassed that I had thought at first that it was about me, that it took me that long to make the connection. But only by putting myself in front of Jesus, then taking some time to walk quietly and reflect, was I able to allow the Spirit to take my prayers to a deeper level. By listening to my friend, then listening to God, I was able to receive direction in how to pray for her.

So I walked and prayed. I apologized for being just the littlest bit self-absorbed. Then I thought of my friend. I didn't tell Jesus how to fix her or what miracle she needed God to perform. I just pictured her, and I pictured me bringing her "right in front of Jesus." I had the picture from scripture of the man on the mat being lowered through the roof. I pictured my friend on a mat, and I pictured myself carrying her to Jesus. Through my day, whenever I thought of her or that verse, I just prayed, "Jesus, I'm putting her right in front of you." I called another mutual friend who knew a bit about the situation and, without revealing any details, simply asked her to be praying as well, since more than one friend brought the paralytic to Jesus.

Notice that God didn't give me a three-point plan, a "word" that I should go and tell my friend about how to live her life. I did tell her what God had told me, and how I was praying for her, putting her right in front of Jesus. I think it may have been helpful to her, a little. I know it was more helpful than any advice would have been.

That day, I think God also had a gift for me—a little demonstration about how to pray for someone by being present—present to them and present to God, all at the same time. Being present is what listening prayer is all about, as we'll explore in the next chapter.

Why are Jesus and the Bible both called "the Word"? Is the Word "intimately and vitally involved" in your life? What does that (or would that) look like in practical terms?

How do you respond to stories? How do stories create readiness for insight? Do you think your heart is receptive to the truth Jesus wants to share with you?

What do you meditate on? What challenges your ability to give anything your "sustained attention"?

You may want to go back and read the whole parable of the sower in Matthew 13. What does it mean to hear and "take in" the good news of the Bible? Does that type of receiving typically go through your head or your heart? What kind of harvest do you think Jesus is talking about?

What would it take to have "unhurried time" in your life? What would you have to say no to? Do you believe it is possible? How can you practice "attentive listening" as you read the Bible?

CHAPTER VIII

Listening in Prayer

Each night when I tuck them into bed, my children say their prayers. Sometimes they will ask me to pray, and I do so gladly, letting them know through my heartfelt words how grateful I am for each of them. When they pray, they say virtually the same words each night, although I have not taught them specific words to recite. My daughter Melanie usually quickly rattles off: "Dear Jesus, Thanks for this day. Thank you for mommy, daddy, Aaron (her brother), Jack (the dog), Cuff and Link (the pet turtles). Give me a good night's sleep, no bad dreams, and a good day tomorrow. Amen." Aaron's prayer is quite similar. Sometimes they will intercede on their own behalf regarding an upcoming spelling test or soccer match.

I love that my children's prayers are full of gratitude and the assumption that this good day has indeed come from God's hand, not some blind luck. But I long for them to truly communicate with him, to pour out their hearts and listen for his answers. Melanie sometimes tells me she prays silently before she falls asleep. I am praying that my gentle instructions on sharing all her worries and fears with God are easier for her to express in the silence of her own heart. I am praying that her Heavenly Father touches her tender heart with his love and reassurances. Aaron is a child who loves solitude and spends lots of time drawing and pondering. I pray that he will learn to listen in the silence that he already loves.

Prayer is communication with God, which hopefully leads to deep communion with God. Ideally, there is mutuality in that communication—a dialogue rather than simply a monologue or meaningless recitation of words.

When we first learn to pray, we pray like children. We do most of the talking. We are in a child-parent relationship with God. That's not bad. In fact, Jesus said that we ought to think of God as a loving Father; we ought to humble ourselves like children that he longs to gather under his wings like a mother hen. We are children of God. Still, when it comes to conversation with God, there is a difference between childlikeness and childishness. A humble, childlike spirit is one that listens. Our childlikeness prompts our humility. When we are childlike, we remember that we are loved, not for our accomplishments but simply because we are. We are aware of our limitations and humbled by them. In fact, just as my children ask me to pray for them, we can ask the Spirit to pray for us, as the Bible promises.

A childish attitude, on the other hand, comes when we are blind to our limitations. We don't realize how small we are. Childish prayer sounds like a three-year-old who has recently mastered new words and language and simply talks nonstop. Childish prayers operate from the motto, "It's all about me." Sometimes we babble like toddlers, asking "Why?" every minute and saying "No!" and "Mine!" quite frequently. Sometimes we are more like sullen teenagers talking (*sigh!*) to their parents, in monosyllables, barely hiding our resentment. We demand to know why things are as they are, why all our friends get to do things that we don't get to; it's just so unfair.

The Apostle Paul wrote to the church at Ephesus about the process of maturing in Christ. "Then we will no longer be infants, tossed back and forth by the waves, and blown here and there by every wind of teaching. . . . Instead, speaking the truth in love, we will in all things grow up into him who is the Head, that is, Christ" (Ephesus 4:14–15). Our growth, our ability to grow up, hinges on whom we are going to listen to. Are we going to listen to God, or someone else?

As we grow, we begin to listen to God, to what he is calling us to. And as we listen, we continue in and nourish our growth, which in turn again enables us to become better listeners. We begin to relate to God in a more adult way, listening and speaking, actually engaging in communication. We're still his children, but we're maturing children who are developing our ability to listen and discern truth.

Communication is an interchange between my self and someone other than my self. There is a distance between us, even if that distance is bridged by clear understanding, by sharing ideas and thoughts and feelings. The gap shrinks as our honesty and vulnerability deepen. But it is impossible to be vulnerable if you don't really believe anyone is listening. It's hard to be honest with someone who isn't there, or at least, you don't think they are. Honesty assumes an expectation of someone hearing us, responding to our exposing of our soul with acceptance, love, and understanding. That is not too much to expect from God.

How do I do that? How do I move from monologue to dialogue and, from there, to even deeper connection with God? By listening.

How do we apply the discipline of listening to prayer? It would seem that listening shares the same type of relationship with prayer that it does with other spiritual practices: if we listen while praying, it takes the experience to a much deeper level, transforms it from a monologue into a dialogue. It opens up the possibility that we would hear God, and if we are brave, we would obey him.

I think the idea of listening prayer (also called contemplative prayer) can be frightening. I know of people who have twisted truth for their own purposes, put words in God's mouth that were obviously not from God. It's also scary because I wonder how do I know, of all those little voices (including the voices of guilt, fear, or even wishful thinking) in my head, which is God's?

> *Contemplative prayer is one of the practices that gives God time and access to work in our inner person, changing the attitudes of the heart that ultimately drive us. A changed heart (Matthew 7:17) can't help but produce "good things out of the good stored up in his heart."*
>
> —JAN JOHNSON[1]

My thoughts do lots of thinking on their own. They range far and wide, wandering down rabbit trails of my mind. While it is possible for God to guide my thoughts, he certainly does not have control over all my thoughts. So not all my thoughts come from him. The problem, of course, is discerning which thoughts are from God and which ones are not.

I am the type of person who comes up with ideas all the time, but I have trouble following through on them. I used to worry about this, until I realized that there was no way on earth I could possibly follow through on even half the ideas that flit through my brain. I had to listen and let the ideas simmer, and see which ones were aligned with God's calling on my life.

It's a matter of balancing trust and discernment. Do I trust God to speak? Do I trust myself enough to listen, to be able to discern his voice? That is also part of the growing-up process, and it is a process that takes a lifetime.

◡ When I Get to Heaven . . . ◡

The Apostle Paul, in writing to a young, rather immature church in the decadent city of Corinth, urged them to love unselfishly. His oft-quoted words—"Love is patient, love is kind . . ."—appear in the thirteenth chapter of his first epistle to them.

A few verses later, he points out that we may not be able to love perfectly, because growth is a process. He seems to be telling this group of believers that the most important thing is to love God and love each other. But you won't always get it exactly right. We are all in the process of spiritual formation, and it won't be completed until we are in heaven.

He writes:

> For we know in part and we prophesy in part, but when perfection comes, the imperfect disappears. When I was a child, I talked like a child. I thought like a child, I reasoned like a child. When I became a man, I put childish ways behind me. Now we see but a poor reflection; then we shall see face to face. Now I know in part; then I shall know fully even as I am fully known [1 Corinthians 13:9–12].

We are all in process. Some of the process has already happened, Paul says. I'm not a child anymore. I'm growing up. Some of the process is yet to come: we don't see truth, we don't see God, in a completely clear way. The King James version that I memorized as a child puts it, "Now we see through a glass darkly."

But we do see. Maybe the glass is not crystal clear, but it is glass, not a brick wall. We don't know God or truth fully, but we do know it in part. And what we don't know, we can ask about. We can put away childish things, like saying, "I just don't get it. It's not fair." We can take God up on his offer when he says, "Come, let us reason together."

I have had countless conversations with people, injured or disappointed in this life, who say, "When I get to heaven, I'm going to ask God . . . " They want to know why they had pain, why their church splintered, why their spouse was unfaithful, why children get cancer, why priests or others claiming to be God's representatives have abused their power. Why, why, why?

I have another why question: Why do we have to wait until we get to heaven to ask these questions?

Why not ask them now?

Paul is not telling us to wait in some celestial waiting room until we can get to see God face-to-face. This whole chapter of the Bible is about love: how love endures, what real love looks like; how "love does not delight in evil but rejoices with the truth" (v. 6). Paul tells his little Corinthian flock to keep seeking that love. Keep loving others. As we seek love, we will want to know more about the source of real love. I know in part, and engaging in conversation with God will help me to know more, and love more.

Prayer is about conversing with God, asking him the things you really want to know right now. That's what I mean by living the questions. We say we'll wait to ask God things face-to-face because we have a nagging sense that once we get to heaven, we'll be able to see the big picture, the other side of the tapestry God is weaving (as a popular metaphor goes), and we will actually understand a little better the things that don't make sense. At least, we hope so. But now, we don't think it's possible to see the big picture. Or we don't want to see it. Sometimes, "living the questions" means having enough faith to just accept that we just don't know the answers.

If we ask now about injustice or pain, it's scary, because it might bring us face-to-face with our doubts. Our faith is sometimes not very strong, and we don't want to test it by bringing up something we're uncertain about. We also might be afraid that if we ask God to correct some injustice, he might throw the ball back in our court. We're terrified that God might want us to change in order to do something about it. If I wait until I'm in heaven to ask God about why children are dying of AIDS, I can put off listening to his call to do something about it—to sponsor one of those children through a relief organization, to visit children in a hospital, to take some small but important action. If I say I'm going to lodge a complaint about my church and its fallible leaders when I get to heaven, I don't have to take steps to be an agent of truth-telling, reconciliation, and forgiveness *now*.

We can ask things of God right now, and he will listen. If we listen to him, he may give us answers, or he may not. We may not like the answers; we may not fully understand them. Asking now requires that we must continue to grapple with issues. It may be that we don't get to go, "Oh, I get it!" and have everything all neatly wrapped up, like the ending of a good mystery novel. We have to embrace the incompleteness of life; we have to live in the unknown. In other words, we have to trust. We sometimes have to wait in the ambiguity of life. Unfortunately for many of us, our religious upbringing has not given us the tools to handle this very well.

This process of deepening our understanding may go on for all of our lives. Mystery is part of the spiritual life. Still, we don't need to put off honesty. We can have conversations with God about our disappointments and pain right now. We don't have to wait.

∿ The Circle of Prayer ∿

In his book *Whole Prayer*, Walter Wangerin points out that in our communication of prayer, "We talk *with* God, not just *to* him. God talks with us, too, causing a circle to be whole and closed between us."[2]

He identifies four parts of the circle of whole prayer:

But if we have never learned the fourth, if we are too impatient and unsubmissive to watch and to wait upon the Lord, then we will never even know that the second and third acts have been accomplished. Without our truly listening, prayer will seem to have failed because communication, remaining incomplete, did in fact fail. The circle stayed broken, and love was left unknown.

Learn the circle. Trust in God to listen and to speak, and our own listening will follow as easily as the eyes of a child follow her father—in whom is all her good.

—WALTER WANGERIN[3]

- "First, we speak,
- while second, God listens.
- Third, God speaks
- while, fourth, we listen."

These four parts often "occur in such swift succession that the complete prayer is revealed as a single, unbroken event," he notes. Unfortunately, we sometimes talk at God and never listen for his reply. We don't really have conversation unless we know how to listen. But listening is something we need to practice, to learn. To do so requires unhurried time and a patient spirit. Since we are often bereft of both of these things, we skip the last phase of prayer, making it incomplete and unsatisfying.

Communication requires give and take, and it doesn't happen fully unless we listen. But our willingness to listen in prayer depends, not just on what we do but who we are.

∿ The Object of God's Affection ∿

What prompts us to seek God, to speak and hope he hears us? Perhaps we think it is the emptiness of our lives without him, that God-shaped vacuum in our souls, our desire for meaning and significance.

Okay, yes. But where does our desire for God come from? Are we seeking or responding? Do we start the conversation or does God?

"Like the spiritual life itself, prayer is initiated by God," Marjorie Thompson writes. "No matter what we think about the origin of our prayers, they are all a response to the hidden workings of the Spirit within. God's desire for us ignites the spark of our desire for God."[4]

When I feel a desire to pray, it is God's spirit that stirs up that desire in the first place. Think about that: God initiates and seeks you out. In my particular religious tradition, the emphasis is on my seeking, my quest for truth and knowledge, my acceptance of truth. It is very easy to assume that it is somehow my acceptance of Jesus, rather than his acceptance of me, that saves me.

While I certainly can't call myself anything without some sort of belief or faith on my part, it's dangerous to assume that my destiny is in my own hands.

Knowing that God is the initiator takes some of the pressure off. Instead of worrying about what I'm doing (am I praying enough, am I praying correctly?), I can focus on who I am and who God is. I am God's beloved child. God is my loving heavenly parent, my dearest friend, my companion, and leader—all at once. God cares enough about me to initiate conversation and relationship. I am the beloved. I am not just the seeker, I am the sought. I am the object of God's affection. It's a truth that demands a response.

Henri Nouwen's classic book, *Life of the Beloved,* was originally written for a friend who wanted Henri to write about the spiritual life for him and his friends. Something clear and simple, without jargon or things he couldn't understand, that would net it out for him, give him the main point of what Christian spirituality was about.

So Henri took up the challenge. "Dear Friend," he wrote, "being the Beloved is the origin and the fulfillment of the life of the Spirit."

Spiritual life is not, at its essence, about *doing* prayer, or *doing* good deeds, or even *learning* how to listen. It is all about "*being* the Beloved." It is about being rather than doing. Our identity is far more critical to our spiritual development than our accomplishments. But how do we put on this identity? How do we become? In a "doing" culture, we think we could learn to just "be" if someone would give us five easy steps!

"As long as 'being the Beloved' is little more than a beautiful thought or a lofty idea that hangs above my life to keep me from becoming depressed, nothing really changes," Nouwen writes. "What is required is to become the Beloved in the commonplaces of my daily existence and bit by bit, to close the gap that exists between what I know myself to be and the countless specific realities of everyday life."[5]

Prayer is where I allow God access to the "commonplaces of my daily existence" and listen to his guidance and advice on those areas. By listening, I transform myself from someone who just has a nice idea that keeps me a little hopeful, to actually embracing my identity as one who is not just loved, but is the beloved.

As God's Beloved, I am not just someone who has mastered some good listening techniques. I am the Beloved. I have received love, heard God's voice calling me Beloved, and made that part of my identity. I am a listener. Because of God's love for me, I want to hear his loving words. God has initiated a relationship with me and put a desire in my soul, and I long to listen. I want God's Spirit with me all the time, guiding me.

If I say I really need to talk with you, and you care about me, you will hopefully say yes, let's sit and talk. And then, what would you do? You would look at me, and say—nothing. You would simply wait for me to tell you whatever it was that I wanted to tell you, right? You might prompt me with a simple question like, "What's going on?" Your body language, your eyes, might communicate care and concern and attentiveness. But you'd be quiet. You wouldn't say, "Where are you? What do you want? What are you trying to say to me?" If you did say these things, I wouldn't speak. I'd wait for you to settle down and just be quiet before I began to respond.

As we talked, you might ask questions to respond and clarify, but you would begin with silence, with quiet attendance.

What would happen to your conversations with God if you used this approach in prayer? If you just waited, attentively and quietly, for him to speak? What would happen to you, to your soul? In other words, would your prayer life change if you went from just using prayer techniques to actually being a prayer listener?

∿ Becoming a Listener ∿

We are hungry for techniques because we think if we just learn the right formula, the right words, we will get a clear connection with God. We won't have to wonder if he's actually hearing us or if we are truly hearing him.

Techniques can be helpful, especially at first. But as our relationship with God develops, we want more. We need more. Conversation with God involves so much more than methods. Because the methods are always distinct from our real selves. There is me, and then, separately, there is the technique. Someone who practices good listening strategies may become good at listening. But beyond just learning a skill, we come to a place where we are changed, transformed into someone who is a good listener. What exactly is the difference between the two?

One person has a skill set, but the other has an identity. She *is* a good listener. It's part of who she is, not just something she can do. We become the beloved; we become a listener.

Real listeners notice. They pay attention. Sometimes we think of prayer exclusively in terms of telling God what should be.

But prayer is more about simply noticing what is—not just during time we've designated for prayer, but all through the day. Noticing the blessings around us, or noticing that challenges seem to be piling up with unprecedented frequency. Noticing the sin in our own hearts some days, the growth on better days. Noticing things to be thankful for, things to ask questions about. Noticing God in circumstances, in creation, in the faces of your loved ones, in his words in your heart, his presence. Noticing the truth about myself, and being able to say what is true and ask for help in changing it.

"How much love God lavishes on each particular heart when he murmurs words intended for that heart alone!" Walter Wangerin notes. "How much love the lonely heart misses if it will not hear the personal word. . . . The Lakota Indians have said to their children *Wachin ksapa yo!* It means, 'Be attentive.' Have an attitude of constant awareness, for God may suddenly speak in any thing of his creation."[6]

Though my mother didn't say, "*Wachin ksapa yo!*" to me, she may as well have. She taught me how to be attentive to God's word in his creation. When I was young, my family lived in the Chicago suburbs. Winters were long and our house was small. My mother, who loves nature with a passion bordering on obsession, would get a little stir-crazy being cooped up in our little ranch house with my brother and me. So at least once a week, even in winter, we would drive a few miles in our beige Volkswagen bug to the local forest preserve. We would hike the nature trail, feed the mallards in the river, and look at the raccoons and other pitiful creatures caged in a small zoo of sorts on the property. More importantly, we would play outside. My brother and I would run through the woods and find leaves and rocks or play in the snow. Eventually, we'd slow down and just walk in the quiet of the woods. My mother would stroll behind us, enjoying the beauty of the trees, the sounds of the birds. She'd occasionally point out different types of birds or warn us about poison ivy. She tells me now that it was simply relaxing, a release for her that was also good for us, a cure for cabin fever. It calmed all of us. In a way, she was listening to God, or perhaps asking him for the strength to get through one more day with two small, rowdy children.

At the time, Mom probably didn't think I was listening, but I was. I was listening to my life and noticing how being in a natural setting, even in the outskirts of Chicago (an area hardly renowned for its natural beauty), brought peacefulness and calm. I witnessed how she was attentive, how she prayed by breathing in the peace of the woods, even though she never said a word about it, even if she didn't consciously think of it as prayer. (Responding in a positive way to that feeling so common to young moms—*I've got to get out of this house!*—is indeed listening prayer.)

All my life, when I have been restless or needed to find God, I have gone to the woods. I listened to my life with my family as a child. When we went camping, hiking, or walking in the woods, we were connected, both to each other and to God, somehow. I felt safe and peaceful. I experienced God more deeply when I looked at and walked through his creation. I am aware of this because I listened to my life. But I must take what God has told me about myself—that I can connect deeply with him by looking at fall trees or watching a hawk soar—and do something with that information, just as my mother did. I must respond by putting myself outside on a regular basis where I can listen for more of him. For me, being outside is a way of conversing with God, but I must actually show up for that conversation to take place.

Listening is a skill; paying attention is something we can practice. Still, what matters more than what we do is who we are. We are God's children, wholly and completely loved. This identity transforms our actions. We are indwelt by the Spirit, who prays on our behalf when we don't have adequate words or even when we fool ourselves into thinking that we do have adequate words.

That being said, we still need to begin with some skills. They are the foundation, the disciplines that will transform us into being good listeners. When we listen in prayer, we begin by quieting our hearts and reminding ourselves, not of how to pray but of who we are: deeply loved children who have the privilege of speaking to and listening to God.

∿ Learning to Listen ∿

So, how do we listen to someone who does not speak in an audible voice?

Part of our hesitation and uncertainty comes from that tendency we have to assume God is limited by space, time, and matter in the same ways that we are. We assume he looks and speaks like a monk, like an old man, or maybe in spiritual psychobabble, or in words we don't really understand, like Deepak Chopra.

The fact is, God is beyond the physical limitations and parameters of our world. He is not an old man with a white beard and a booming voice. God can communicate in ways that we can't. God can guide our thoughts without speaking aloud. John Ortberg explains this so clearly in his book *The Life You've Always Wanted:*

> To "speak" to someone is simply to direct their thoughts toward something. Because you are reading these words, you are thinking a series of thoughts that you would not be thinking otherwise. Your thoughts are being led by another person.
>
> Because I am a finite human being, I have to use indirect means to guide your thoughts. I must express ideas in words

so you can hear them or read them. I need to give them some physical form in order to communicate with you.

But God does not. God can directly guide my thoughts without the aid of intervening sounds or images.[7]

Listening to God is, in some ways, like listening to any other person. We need to be quiet and pay attention in order to hear what is being said.

When I pray, I begin by simply breathing. I have to breathe anyway, but how I breathe makes a difference. If I slowly breathe in and out, I begin to feel calmer. I love that in both Hebrew and Greek, the original languages of the Bible, the same word can be used for Spirit and for breath (*ruach* in Hebrew, *pnema* in Greek).

I say these words quietly, reminding myself that God's Spirit is as close as the air I breathe. I breathe in God. Then I just wait. I usually have to remind myself, "I am not in a hurry."

As Thompson writes, "Attending to the moment of encounter is crucial." I want to be present to the presence of God. It is easy to rush into prayer with a shopping list of needs and wants, and I try to be deliberate about not doing that.

Then I listen. Sometimes, thoughts come. Sometimes, what I have read in scripture or another book will come to mind. I make a regular habit of reading scripture and other thought-provoking books. Sometimes, these will prompt a conversation with God. Often when I sit in the morning to listen, I will watch the sunrise, I will look at the trees in the backyard or the vegetables in the garden.

I usually write in a journal. This can be an excellent way to converse with God. I often start my day by just writing down the thoughts and bits of dreams that are in my head. What worries me? What did I dream about? I think sometimes God reveals us to ourselves in our dreams, so if I get it down on paper, without trying to interpret what the dreams mean, I can put it on the table, so to speak, with God. Sometimes I'll go back through my journal and see what God has done with the things that troubled me yesterday or last month. Usually, I see more clearly how he's working in my life by just noticing where I've been.

Then I simply get quiet and listen. If I think God is speaking, I will jot notes in my journal. I sometimes just sit in silence, not needing words. I imagine God sitting right next to me, simply being, simply loving. I try to receive this as the gift that it is.

I don't have a set routine beyond this, although I may do any of the following: read a psalm and pray it out loud to God, listen to God though scripture, take a walk, write a prayer in my journal.

This morning I sat in silence for a while, making a few notes in my journal. Then chaos descended the staircase in the form of my two children. I made their lunches, talked with them (and listened to them!) around the breakfast table, made sure they packed up their books and got out the door. Soon after, I walked with the dog. It was a beautiful October day. The sky was bright blue and full of small, round, wispy, swirled clouds that looked like the downy curls on a baby's head.

A small maple tree along the sidewalk was brilliant yellow. I stopped and walked up to it, looking up through the leaves and simply enjoying the beauty of the yellow leaves against the sky. The tree was petite, so its main fork was about six inches above my eye level. I turned my gaze from the leaves to the tree's trunk and saw a small bird's nest in the alcove created by the fork of the tree. I looked up again, watching some of the leaves fall around me. I just felt joyful, experiencing the beauty of the earth, the sky, the tree. I love that God gives the trees beautiful colors that don't clash with the sky. I love that he made trees just right for holding little nests and hard-wired little bird brains with directions for nest-building. Thus part of my prayer time today involved standing next to a tree and noticing God's handiwork in it.

◡ Listening Prayer ◡

Jesus' disciples got to watch him model life with God for them. They noticed him being kind to the poor, saw him including and welcoming the marginalized, knew he got up early many times to spend time in solitude. They were aware of how well he knew the scriptures and how he spoke words of wisdom, how God's power flowed through him in miraculous ways.

But the one thing that really caught their attention was how he prayed. He must have done something different from the other rabbis of his day. He wasn't just saying words. He was communing with his Father.

"One day Jesus was praying in a certain place. When he finished, one of his disciples said to him, 'Lord, teach us to pray, just as John taught his disciples'" (Luke 11:1).

And Jesus responds: call him Daddy. Abba. A term of both endearment and deep respect. He invites his disciples to not just say words but to enjoy the intimacy with the Father that he himself enjoyed. It's likely that Jesus' prayer, which focused on honoring God and forgiving others, might have been different from what John the Baptist or other teachers taught their disciples.

Jesus gave his disciples some words: "Our Father (Abba), hallowed be your name" (Luke 11:2). But the words were not what was important (although people have made them perhaps too important). Later in the chapter Luke records this comment from Jesus: "Ask, it will be given to you; seek and you will find; knock and the door will be opened to you" (Luke 11:9).

In other words, when you pray, expect a response. Talk to God, seek him out, knock on the door, and then *listen*. He will respond. Jesus continued: "Which of you fathers, if your son asks for a fish, will give him a snake instead? Or if he asks for an egg, will give him a scorpion? If you then, though you are evil, know how to give good gifts to your children, how much more will your Father in heaven give the Holy Spirit to those who ask him!" (Luke 11:11–13).

When we pray, we should focus on God. We should ask him for each day's needs, yes. But the focus of our prayers should be on the relationship of intimacy. And God will give the Spirit to us— he will put his Spirit in us. Sometimes, that can take us to a place beyond words, where we are simply with God, in silence, in communion. Letting go of having to come up with something brilliant or profound to say can be both freeing and humbling.

Because contemplative prayer is one where we simply enjoy God's presence and don't fill the space with words, it is easiest to practice it in silence and solitude. It is very hard if you are a control freak.

I find I have to fight the urge to try to reel God in with more words, to talk "at" him, hoping he'll come over and do what I want him to. I have to let go of control, to simply say, I want to listen, God. Speak to me. And, even more challenging, I have to just be quiet and listen.

> *Reliance on our own thoughts and words, even in our praying, can be one facet of a need to control things, to set the agenda, or at least to know what the agenda is even in our relationship with God. It is in silence that we habitually release our own agendas and our need to control and become more willing and able to give ourselves to God's loving initiative.*
>
> —RUTH BARTON[8]

It's easy to pray prayers that are sort of like e-mails to God: here's what I think; here's what I need. That type of communication is okay, but if I want to cultivate that relationship, that intimacy, I need more than e-mail. I need sitting-on-the-front-porch-holding-hands type of conversation—where I can just be with God. We can be quiet together, we can talk together, and most importantly, we are not hurried.

We can converse with God in this way. We can complete what Wagernin called the "circle of prayer" by listening, by shifting our focus from our own needs and concerns to simple contemplation.

What is contemplative prayer? It is simple, yet profound. Have you ever contemplated anything? Of course you have. You contemplate your next move in chess. You contemplate a sunset or a sunrise, or perhaps an artistic masterpiece. You contemplate your reflection in a mirror, wonder-

> *Prayer as conversation with God can be deeply fulfilling. However, if it is the only form our prayer takes, we may begin to sense that something is missing. There are two reasons for this. First, prayer is by nature, more than conversation. To limit its concept to dialogue is to allow some of the most profound expressions of prayer to escape our notice. Second, our "conversation" may, in practice, be less a dialogue than a monologue that borders on talking at God.*
>
> —MARJORIE THOMPSON[9]

ing if that shirt really goes with the pants or if others will find you attractive. You think about it, behold it, let it come to you, speak to you.

Contemplative prayer is simply beholding God, listening to him, noticing what comes to you.

One technique for moving from just conversation to a deeper listening contemplation is called centering prayer. It has been used for centuries.

You need to find a place that is quiet, where you will not be disturbed. This may be your biggest hurdle, but don't give up. Once you are alone, begin by getting comfortable, sitting upright with your feet on the floor. Find a position that is comfortable but in which you can stay alert. For a few moments, simply be still and let go of your wildly wandering thoughts.

Once you've quieted down a bit, select a name for God that feels intimate. What do you usually call him? Lord, Abba, Father, Spirit?

Those who practice contemplative prayer get used to waiting on God in expectant alertness. Because God is liable to answer questions asked in contemplative prayer anywhere in life, we stay alert beyond the official moments of prayer. The waiting is active—being fully present to each person and circumstance, convinced that God is on the move, wanting to be there to see what happens. It is as open ended as wordless contemplation. You don't know exactly what will come, only that God is present.

—JAN JOHNSON[10]

From there, sit quietly and think about what it is that you truly need. Mercy, grace, wisdom, guidance? Combine your name for God and your deepest need into a single sentence. A classic is, "Lord Jesus, have mercy on me." You may want to use "Spirit, guide me" or some other short petition.

This is also known as a "breath prayer" because it can be said in the space of a single breath. Simply focus on God using that sentence. Do not vainly repeat it over and over as a mantra. That's not the idea. Rather, this one-sentence prayer is a way to remind yourself to focus on God when your mind wanders. The goal is to simply be with God, to simply contemplate him—looking, watching, loving. You can take the prayer with you in your day, and when you feel you need it, simply take a few deep, slow breaths, and pray. Then listen.

Beyond communication with God is the deeper experience of communion. Here we are no longer acting childishly. Instead, we are relating to God as we would to a deep friend or a lover, someone who knows us intimately and with whom we can feel comfortable just being quiet, just experiencing each other's presence. It is this type of relationship that God is inviting each of us into. We move toward this experience by listening, rather than speaking, because it is God's initiative that makes such connection possible.

We may or may not feel that connection right away. Just sitting in silent prayer will train our ear to listen for God's still, small voice. But we must be patient and learn what it is we are listening for. This will take time. Our awareness of God's presence may come later, even the next day. It may not come in the form of specific instructions but more as a reassurance that we are within God's will.

If I am expecting directions about things to do, I'm often disappointed. Usually what comes to me when I practice contemplative prayer is just reassurance that I am loved, that God is with me. As I said before, it's more about being than doing. He's aware of me, much more than I am aware of him. This doesn't inspire guilt but, rather, amazement and love.

I'm learning how to stop asking, "What do you want me to do?" and moving toward simply asking, "What do you want me to know?" I love asking that because God most often answers it with a simple phrase: "I want you to know that I love you."

You may or may not experience this when you first begin to try listening in prayer. Don't give up. Realize that expectations are a burden you should set down before you spend time in contemplative prayer.

Trust that God will transform, not only your prayers but your spirit as you listen to him. As you continue to listen, may you continue to find God in the story of your life.

How do you feel about the idea of God working on your "inner person"? How might listening prayer create space for God to change your heart?

Have you ever prayed and felt disconnected from God? Do you ever wonder if he heard you, if he loved you? Is it possible that you missed what he wanted to tell you, that his "love was left unknown"?

Are you willing to let God speak? Are you willing to let his words be more important than yours? What would it look like to release your agenda and let God initiate?

Do you ever sense that "something is missing" in your prayer life? Do you have the sense that God seems distant? How can you begin to move from conversation to contemplation?

How would you have to live your life "beyond the official moments of prayer" in order to be attentive to God? What do you think Johnson means by "active waiting" on God? What would that look like in your life?

Epilogue

One of the greatest challenges of my life is simply the task of paying attention, of understanding what my life, in its ordinary moments, is about. What is God saying to me through my life, through other people, in the spaces that I try to create for him through simple practices like listening prayer?

I desire to hear God, in part because I simply want to communicate with the lover of my soul. If God is a lover, in the purest, kindest sense of that word, wouldn't I want to listen to him?

I want to feel a sense of purpose and calling. Sometimes I do feel it, or at least think I'm hearing and actually following God. Then other voices distract or discourage me. I forget to listen to God, and instead I am listening to well-intentioned but misguided friends, the voice of my own insecurity, or the demands of my busy life.

"There is a divine Abyss within us all, a holy Infinite Center, a Heart, a Life who speaks in us and through us to the world," Thomas Kelly wrote.

We have all heard this holy Whisper at times. At times we have followed the Whisper, and amazing equilibrium of life, amazing effectiveness of living set in. But too many of us have heeded the Voice only at times. Only at times have we submitted to His holy guidance. We have not counted this Holy Thing within us to be the most precious thing in the world.[1]

You have heard this holy Whisper at times. I know you have. I know I have, and it is indeed connected with a sense of purpose and effectiveness. Like me, I'm guessing that you want to hear it more often, and more clearly—clearly enough that you will have the courage to respond to it, to converse with the One who whispers, and to allow that divine conversation to change your life.

I hope you will take some steps to live out the ideas we've explored in this book, to begin to pay attention to your life. God is intimately involved in your story, and if you listen, you will find him in it. You can hear his "holy whispers."

If you find that challenging, the following "life review" exercise may be helpful. This is a time-tested method of self-examination that will help you develop your ability to notice God.

On a large sheet of blank paper, draw a timeline for your life. Divide it into five- or ten-year increments. For each five- or ten-year period, write or draw something that tells how you saw yourself and how you saw God. What were the spiritual milestones in your life? What things did you say to yourself in various seasons? (For example, did you say, "I'm lucky," or "I'm special," or perhaps, "I'm not good enough"?) What things did you think God said to you? Maybe you didn't know him as a child, but he knew you. He was whispering to you, even if you think you didn't hear it. In occasional moments of longing or joy, you may have sensed it, but you just didn't have anyone to name it for you. But you can name it now. In those moments, God was making you aware of himself. He was calling you to himself, even if you did not recognize it, even if you still aren't sure. This simple exercise will help you to find God in the story of your life.

God is not just in our past but also in our present and our future. Knowing your story allows you to go with God from this point forward in a journey of discovery, to keep listening and noticing, to continue the conversation.

What would that look like? Here's an example. I told you I keep bumping into people who want to write. I have this growing desire to teach writing. A few months ago, I had a chance conversation with one of my professors from my alma mater, Wheaton College. We chatted; she listened to what I was doing, careerwise. She asked if I'd ever thought about teaching writing. Well, yes, as a matter of fact, I had. I should not have been surprised. She told me that I ought to consider teaching at a college level (an idea that stirred a strong emotional response in me). But in order to do so, I would need a master's degree (which I don't yet have).

A month later I was working on a magazine article and interviewed an English professor at another college. We got talking about teaching and writing and literature. I just had another conversation with him on the phone this morning, in which he gave me some great advice about master's programs, what colleges are looking for, what sort of teaching jobs are out there, and so on.

I'm going to continue to investigate looking at what it would take to pursue this. I am walking forward, listening, letting God lead, letting his grace take me where he wants me to go. The story is still unfolding, but I'm simply trying to listen and to obey when he prompts me to move forward. I don't know what God's going to do or where he's going to take me, but I'm simply trying to listen and walk forward through the adventure as he directs.

So keep listening to the story of your life. And also, listen to other people. Engage in the ministry of listening. Through others, you will hear God speak to you, and you will also be Christ to them. Community is built through the ministry of listening to others—and not just other believers. Listening to people who are questioning God's very existence helps them to discover God in their story but also helps us clarify our own thinking and faith.

This happened to me when I took a year off from Wheaton, starting half-way through my junior year. For two semesters, I attended the University of Pennsylvania, an Ivy League school in urban Philadelphia, where the student population was 60 percent Jewish and the rest, except a small handful, appeared to be atheists. (Some were Jewish atheists, which made for very interesting discussions.)

Both institutions were a key part of my story, and I learned a lot at each. But listening and conversing with people who questioned my faith at Penn, who said things like, "How can you call yourself an intellectual and believe in God?" really helped me. That may seem odd to you, but it's true. It forced me to consider in a very real way: Was my faith a rational and reasonable thing? Why did I believe what I had grown up believing? Listening respectfully to others, having to articulate a defense for my own beliefs, praying that God would give me words and really listening for his answers—God used these things to teach me about himself and about myself. Listening to others, even those who disagreed with me, brought me to a deeper faith and deeper understanding of myself.

If we pay attention, God will reveal himself in our story. He will give us the wisdom to understand the story of our life and find him in it.

As Paul wrote to the Ephesians, "I keep asking that the God of our Lord Jesus Christ, the glorious Father, may give you the Spirit of wisdom and revelation, so that you may know him better" (Ephesians 1:17).

Pray that verse for yourself. Ask God for help in discerning, ask him for that Spirit of wisdom. Like Paul, don't just ask once but "keep asking." And keep listening. That's the whole point of listening, of finding God in your story: to "know him better." Sure, you need to know yourself, but not just so you can be self-aware. It's so that you can be more God-aware. Coming to a place of faith commitment is important, but it doesn't mean we're done seeking, listening, or finding God. Because when you become aware of him, you'll realize that you aren't the only one looking and listening. God is seeking you out as well. He's been a part of your story all along and wants you to know him. God's deep desire for his people, for you, is a loving relationship.

He expressed that desire through his prophet Jeremiah: "'Then you will call upon me and come and pray to me, and I will listen to you. You will seek me and find me when you seek me with all your heart. I will be found by you,' declares the LORD" (Jeremiah 29:12–14). We seek and listen to God; God seeks and listens to us. Together, we write a love story.

Listen to your life; listen to other wise people who can help you discern truth. Spend time in silence, meditation, prayer—all the while, listening to the story God is telling to you, and is telling through you. He's seeking you out; he wants you to seek him as well. God desires to be found by you. He's crafting your story so that you, and all the rest of us, will know him better. Because that's what your story is ultimately about: finding him.

The Author

Keri Wyatt Kent is the author of *God's Whisper in a Mother's Chaos* (IVP, 2000), *The Garden of the Soul* (IVP, 2002), and *Breathe* (Revell, 2005). She has coauthored several books and Bible studies, including *Courageous Faith Through the Year* with Bill Hybels (IVP, 2004). Her writing and teaching ministry is focused on guiding others toward a deeper and more authentic relationship with Christ. A former newspaper reporter, she has been writing professionally for more than twenty years.

Keri has been an active member of Willow Creek Community Church in South Barrington, Illinois, since 1987. She currently teaches spiritual formation classes for women's ministries at Willow. She speaks and leads retreats for MOPS (Mothers of Preschoolers) groups and women's groups at other churches, and has been a workshop speaker at the Hearts at Home women's conference and the MOPS International Convention.

Currently, Keri runs her own freelance writing business. She writes for a number of magazines including *Christian Parenting Today, Today's Christian Woman,* and *Outreach Magazine.* She and her husband Scot have been married for fifteen years and live in the Chicago area with their two children, a dog, and two turtles. Learn more at www.keriwyattkent.com.

References

INTRODUCTION: PAYING ATTENTION

1. Lamott, A. *Bird by Bird.* New York: Doubleday/Anchor Books, 1994, p. 100.

2. Peterson, E. H. (Ed.) *The Message.* Colorado Springs, Colo.: NavPress, 1993. Note that all quotations from the Bible throughout this book have been taken from this edition of *The Message.*

3. Johnson, J. *When the Soul Listens.* Colorado Springs, Colo.: NavPress, 1999, p. 48.

4. Peck, M. S. *The Road Less Traveled.* New York: Simon & Schuster, 1978, pp. 120, 121.

5. Willard, D. *Hearing God.* Downers Grove, Ill.: InterVarsity Press, 1999.

6. Johnson, J. *When the Soul Listens.* Colorado Springs, Colo.: NavPress, 1999, p. 43.

PART ONE: HOLY MOMENTS: LISTENING TO YOUR LIFE

1. Sexton, A. As quoted on www.brainyquote.com, and elsewhere.

2. Palmer, P. *Let Your Life Speak.* San Francisco: Jossey-Bass, 2000, pp. 3, 4.

CHAPTER ONE: WHAT DO I LOVE?

1. Lamott, A. *Bird by Bird,* p. 15.

2. Carter, J. "Building a Better World." *Habitat World* (published by Habitat for Humanity, Americus, Ga.), 2005, *22*(1), 2.

3. Lewis, C. S. "The Weight of Glory." *The Weight of Glory and Other Addresses.* London: William Collins Sons, 1941, pp. 3–4.

4. Nouwen, H. J. M. *Life of the Beloved.* New York: Crossroad Publishing, p. 31.

5. Ortberg, J. *The Life You've Always Wanted.* Grand Rapids, Mich.: Zondervan, 1997, p. 67.

6. Buechner, F. *The Hungering Dark.* San Francisco: HarperSanFrancisco, 1969, p. 31.

7. Buechner, F. *The Hungering Dark,* p. 31.

CHAPTER TWO: HOW HAVE I STRUGGLED?

1. Peck, M. S., *The Road Less Traveled,* p. 15.

2. Beuchner, F. *Whistling in the Dark.* San Francisco: HarperSanFrancisco, 1977.

3. Nouwen, H. J. M. *The Inner Voice of Love.* New York: Doubleday, 1996, p. 26.

4. Kidd, S. M. *When the Heart Waits.* New York: HarperCollins, 1990, p. 13.

5. Rilke, R. M. *Letters to a Young Poet.* New York: Norton, 1934, p. 34.

6. Gire, K. *The Divine Embrace.* Wheaton, Ill.: Tyndale, p. 91.

7. Lewis, C. S. *The Problem of Pain.* New York: MacMillan, 1944, p. 91. (Republished by HarperCollins in 2001.)

8. Gire, K. *Windows of the Soul.* Grand Rapids, Mich.: Zondervan, 1996, p. 194.

CHAPTER THREE: WHAT IS MY DESIRE?

1. Cooney, B. *Miss Rumphius.* New York: Puffin Books, 1982.

2. Eldredge, J. *Waking the Dead.* Nashville, Tenn.: Thomas Nelson Publishers, 2003, p. 95.

3. Wright, V. H. *The Soul Tells a Story.* Downers Grove, Ill.: InterVarsity Press, 2005, p. 102.

4. Casillas, O. "Music Makes the Difference." *Chicago Tribune,* July 26, 2005, p. 1.

5. Eldredge, J. *Waking the Dead,* p. 40.

6. Cameron, J. *The Artist's Way.* New York: Penguin Putnam Inc., 1992, p. 25.

7. Miller, D. *Blue Like Jazz.* Nashville, Tenn.: Thomas Nelson Publishers, 2003, p. 239.

8. Warren, R. *The Purpose-Driven Life.* Grand Rapids, Mich.: Zondervan, 2002, p. 17.

9. Warren, R. *The Purpose-Driven Life,* p. 69.

Chapter Four: Community:
Listening Together

1. Bonhoeffer, D. *Life Together.* New York: HarperCollins, 1954, p. 97.

2. Nouwen, H. J. M. *Life of the Beloved,* p. 26.

3. Mulholland, R. M., Jr. *Invitation to a Journey.* Downers Grove, Ill.: InterVarsity Press, 1993, p. 12.

4. Ping, D., and Clippard, A. *Quick-to-Listen Leaders.* Loveland, Colo.: Group Publishing, 2005, p. 61.

5, Ping, D., and Clippard, A. *Quick-to-Listen Leaders,* p. 16.

6. Fryling, A. *The Art of Spiritual Listening.* Colorado Springs, Colo.: Shaw Books, 2003, p. 21.

Chapter Five: Compassion:
Suffering Together

1. Lewis, C. S. *The Lion, the Witch and the Wardrobe.* New York: MacMillan, 1950, p. 64.

2. Bonhoeffer, D. *Life Together,* p. 23.

3. Fryling, A. *The Art of Spiritual Listening,* p. 20.

CHAPTER SIX: LISTENING IN SILENCE

1. Foster, R. *Celebration of Discipline.* San Francisco: HarperSanFrancisco, 1978, p. 107.

2. Foster, R. *Celebration of Discipline,* p. 98.

3. Barton, R. *Invitation to Solitude and Silence.* Downers Grove, Ill.: InterVarsity Press, 2004, p. 31.

4. Willard, D. *The Spirit of the Disciplines.* New York: HarperCollins, 1988, p. 160.

5. Bonhoeffer, D. *Life Together,* p. 78.

6. Nouwen, H. J. M. "Moving from Solitude to Community to Ministry." *Leadership Journal,* Spring 1995, p. 83.

7. Barton, R. *Invitation to Solitude and Silence,* p. 50.

CHAPTER SEVEN: LISTENING TO SCRIPTURE

1. Peterson, E. H. (Ed.) *The Message.*

2. Mulholland, R. M. *Shaped by the Word.* Nashville, Tenn.: Upper Room Books, 2000, p. 38.

3. Wangerin, W. *Whole Prayer.* Grand Rapids, Mich.: Zondervan, 1998, p. 37.

4. Ortberg, J. *The Life You've Always Wanted,* p. 186.

5. Peterson, E. H. (Ed.) *The Message.*

6. Mulholland, R. M. *Shaped by the Word,* p. 57.

7. Thompson, M. *Soul Feast.* Nashville, Tenn.: John Knox Press, 1995, pp. 18–19.

CHAPTER EIGHT: LISTENING IN PRAYER

1. Johnson, J. *When the Soul Listens,* p. 33.

2. Wangerin, W. *Whole Prayer,* p. 29.

3. Wangerin, W. *Whole Prayer,* p. 29.

4. Thompson, M. *Soul Feast,* p. 31.

5. Nouwen, H. J. M. *Life of the Beloved,* p. 39.

6. Wangerin, W. *Whole Prayer,* p. 35.

7. Ortberg, J. *The Life You've Always Wanted,* p. 139.

8. Barton, R. *Invitation to Solitude and Silence,* p. 35.

9. Thompson, M. *Soul Feast,* p. 32.

10. Johnson, J. *When the Soul Listens,* pp. 106, 107.

EPILOGUE

1. Kelly, T. *A Testament of Devotion.* New York: HarperCollins, 1941, p. 72.

Keri Wyatt Kent
Breathe
Creating Space for God
in a Hectic Life
ISBN: 0-8007-3060-7
256 pgs.
$12.99
Released 5/05

*An Invitation to Make Time for
What Matters Most*

"In this thoughtful book, Keri Wyatt Kent leads us to a place where we can catch our breath—and keep it!"
    —*Elisa Morgan,* president and CEO, MOPS International

Author Keri Wyatt Kent calls to the part of a woman longing to break free from the hectic pace of life. Through "breathing exercises" and personal accounts of women who made lasting changes, you'll discover how to downsize your to-do list, eliminate hurry, and find the rest your soul longs for.